From The Library of

George & Melinda Nalley

Book 2072

Christ's Coming and His Kingdom

D1042539

Christ's Coming and His Kingdom

A Study in Bible Prophecy
by
Keith M. Bailey

John Witherspoon College
Library

Christian Publications, Inc.
Harrisburg, Pennsylvania

Christian Publications, Inc.
25 S. 10th Street, P.O. Box 3404
Harrisburg, PA 17105

The mark of *CP* vibrant faith

ISBN: 0-87509-296-9
Library of Congress Catalog Card Number: 80-70733
© 1981 by Christian Publications, Inc. All rights reserved
Unless otherwise indicated, all Bible quotations are from the *New American Standard Bible,* © The Lockman Foundation 1960, 1962, 1963, 1971, 1972, 1973, 1975, and are used by permission.
Printed in the United States of America

Contents

Introduction

The Second Coming of the Lord Jesus Christ is an article of faith among all who call themselves Christian, but beliefs about the details of His return and the relationship of His return to the kingdom of God divide the church into three major camps: the amillennialists, the postmillennialists, and the premillennialists. One of the key differences centers on interpretation of the thousand-year period mentioned in Revelation 20. The amillennialist does not accept any literal one thousand-year reign of Christ but interprets Revelation 20 to be the present state of the church. This group believes that Christ will come some day, and when He does the general resurrection and the general judgment will take place and eternity will then begin. The postmillennialist believes that the church by revival and aggressive evangelism will bring in the kingdom, and after one thousand years of Christ's blessing Christ will return to terminate history. The premillenarian believes that Christ is coming again and He alone can set up the kingdom. Premillennialists conceive the kingdom to be literal and its duration to be actually one thousand years.

This study is written without apology from the stance of the premillenarian. The position is supported both biblically and historically. First, the premillennial position is most ancient and seems to have been the prevailing view of the ante-Nicene church. The teaching of a literal millennial reign goes back to Justin Martyr and Irenaeus, both of the second century. Phillip Schaff, the eminent church historian, said:

> The most striking point in the eschatology of the ante-Nicene age is the prominent chiliasm, or millenarianism, that is, the belief of a visible reign of Christ in glory on earth with the risen saints for one thousand years before the general resurrection and judgment.[1]

Many early church fathers wrote regarding the millennial hope.

Second, if a doctrine is to have acceptance, it must be both biblical and apostolic. It must be tested by the question, Was it taught in the early church or is it some recent theological innovation? Premillennialism is both biblical and apostolic.

The premillennial position satisfies the expectations of the prophets. Morris A. Inch, chairman of the Department of Biblical Studies at Wheaton College, Wheaton, Illinois, says:

> I personally take the premillennial option. It seems to be the more obvious implication, and it also extends the earthy flavor we find in the prophets, as Isaiah illustrated:
>> Then the eyes of the blind will
>>   be opened,
>> And the ears of the deaf will be
>>   unstopped.
>> Then the lame will leap like a
>>   deer,
>> And the tongue of the dumb
>>   will shout for joy.
>> For waters will break forth in
>>   the wilderness
>> And streams in the desert (Isa. 35:5-6,
>>   NASB).

8

Somehow to translate all this terrestrial imagery into the eternal state seems to do it injustice.

The premillennial view likewise gives the impression of wrapping up history instead of dropping it like a hot potato.[2]

Finally, the theology of premillennialism more than any other system of thought offers a reasonable answer to the conclusions of history and is the only eschatology that seems to square with the realities of the modern world. Harold B. Kuhn, of Asbury Theological Seminary, has this to say about the premillennial philosophy of history:

> Premillennialism, moreover, tries to face the entire range of predicted events which the New Testament seems to indicate will antedate and lead to the consummation of the age. It notes, for example, the preparatory signs of the advent; it believes the end time will be a period of great distress on the earth, a time when men grope for solutions, but without success. It believes there will be a special dealing of God with the Hebrew people, by which they may be led to resettle in their ancient land. Premillennialism feels the rising international lawlessness and increasing manipulation of technical civilization by "strong men" will herald the end time. . . . We have noted that the Christian message implies a characteristic philosophy of history; it necessarily involves a special way of viewing human events and of understanding history. . . . Christianity must interact with the stark facts of history and their display of human depravity in our day.[3]

In the midst of the widespread collapse of the modern

world, the Christian does well to search the Scriptures for comfort and hope. The hope of Christ's coming and His kingdom provides the Christian with the *solace* he needs to live as a stranger in this cosmic system now coming rapidly under judgment. This kingdom message is also his *incentive* to unswerving loyalty to Christ and complete obedience to His mandate for world evangelization. In this the world's darkest night the church has her best opportunity to preach to men the "world to come" and how to prepare for it.

---

1.   Phillip Schaff, *History of the Christian Church*, vol. 2, (Grand Rapids: Wm. B. Eerdmans Publishing Co.) p. 614.

2.   Morris A. Inch, *Understanding Bible Prophecy* (New York: Harper & Row, 1977), p. 103.

3.   Harold B. Kuhn, "The Nature of Last Things," in *Christian Faith and Modern Theology*, ed. Carl F. H. Henry (Grand Rapids: Baker, Reprinted 1971 from original printing by Channel Press, New York), p. 410.

1

The Waiting Community

The church of Jesus Christ stands alone in its expectations of divine intervention in world affairs. The exact form of that intervention the church finds in the Scriptures. The true church is waiting for the literal, personal, visible, and bodily return of Jesus Christ, her risen Lord.

The early church was a waiting church. In his letter to the young church in Thessalonica, Paul wrote:

> *For they themselves ₍the believers in Macedonia and Achaia₎ report about us what kind of a reception we had with you, and how you turned to God from idols to serve a living and true God, and to wait for His Son from heaven, whom He raised from the dead, that is Jesus, who delivers us from the wrath to come (1 Thess. 1:9-10, NASB).*

Because the Spirit of God worked so mightily in that church, it became a great center of evangelism and was a model to all the churches in Asia. The members of the church in Thessalonica had, for the most part, been pagans before their conversion. They had no idea of the moral nature of the true God. They had not read the self-disclosures of God found in His Word. They had no concept of sin. The biblical concept of heaven was strange to them. None of these things had been a part of their lives until the day the gospel was preached in their city. Under the ministry of the Spirit of God, their minds were opened and they turned to Christ. In turning to Christ they turned away from idols.

Their new allegiance was to the true and the living God. From the day of their conversion the Thessalonians began to wait for the return of Christ. Biblical conversion means to turn away from the old life and turn to a new life in Christ. In this passage Paul indicates another dimension to conversion: those who truly turn from idols begin to wait for God's Son from heaven.

The community of Christians were, then, a people waiting for the coming of Christ. What was true for the Christians in Thessalonica was true for all the Christians of the first century—they were a waiting community. They were captivated with the truth that Jesus Christ is coming again.

The Effect on the Assembly Life of the Church

This posture of expectation had a very important bearing on the everyday life of the church. Every aspect of its assembly life marked the church as a waiting community.

First, the *gathering* of the church showed its expectation of Christ's return.

Since therefore, brethren, we have confidence to enter the holy place by the blood of Jesus, by a new and living way which He inaugurated for us through the veil, that is, His flesh, and since we have a great priest over the house of God, let us draw near with a sincere heart in full assurance of faith, having our hearts sprinkled clean from an evil conscience and our bodies washed with pure water. Let us hold fast the confession of our hope without wavering, for He who promised is faithful; and let us consider how to stimulate one another to love and good deeds, not forsaking our own assembling together, as is the habit of some, but encouraging one another; and all the more, as you see the day drawing near (Heb. 10:19-25, NASB).

The writer to the Hebrews exhorted them to meet frequently because the assembly of God's people has a very definite relationship to the coming of the Lord. Since the day of His coming is drawing nigh, believers ought to guard against anything that would keep them from the assembly of the saints. The church gathering is a foretaste of a greater gathering in the future. Paul spoke of the "coming of our Lord Jesus Christ, and our gathering together to Him" (2 Thess. 2:1). That great mass gathering of the people of God will occur when the Lord Jesus himself descends from heaven with a shout, with the voice of an archangel, and with the sound of the trump of God; and the dead in Christ shall rise and we that are alive shall be translated and caught up together with them to meet the Lord in the air (1 Thess. 4:16-17). When the church gathers now, the gathering is to remind God's people of the coming of the Lord. It is to remind us of the rapture. It is to remind us that Christ may catch us off the earth's scene at any time. We should therefore be prepared in our hearts for the coming of the Lord.

One of the most infectious things about apostolic Christianity was its strong expectation of Christ's return. Every assembly was a celebration of the coming of the Lord. This practice needs to be revived. How would today's evangelical church stand up if it were evaluated as the waiting community? Do our assemblies celebrate the fact that the King is coming soon? Every church meeting today should be a dress rehearsal for the rapture. It ought to promote our readiness for the coming of the Lord Jesus at any time.

Second, the ordinance of the *Lord's Supper* is another distinguishing mark of this waiting community called the church.

> *For I received from the Lord that which I also delivered to you, that the Lord Jesus in the night in which He was betrayed took bread; and when He had given thanks, He broke it, and said, "This is My body, which is for you; do this in remembrance of Me." In the same way He took the cup also, after supper, saying, "This cup is the new covenant in My blood; do this, as often as you drink it, in remembrance of Me." For as often as you eat this bread and drink the cup, you proclaim the Lord's death until He comes (1 Cor. 11:23-26, NASB).*

Every time the saints of God come to the table of the Lord to break bread, they are celebrating the coming of Jesus. The Lord's table is a temporary table. It is a substitute for His literal presence. While He is absent in body from us, He has given us the table. The bread and the cup are symbols of His body and His blood, and every time we partake of them we are to contemplate His Second Coming.

Third, the circumstances of the end time call for intense, peculiar *prayer* on the part of the waiting church. Good judgment and a sober spirit are the prerequisites of such a prayer ministry. In 1 Peter 4, the apostle writes a word of instruction to the scattered Christians, many of whom were enduring great persecution.

> *The end of all things is at hand; therefore, be of sound judgment and sober spirit for the purpose of prayer. Above all, keep fervent in your love for one another, because love covers a multitude of*

sins. Be hospitable to one another without com-
plaint. As each one has received a special gift,
employ it in serving one another, as good stew-
ards of the manifold grace of God. Whoever
speaks, let him speak, as it were, the utterances
of God; whoever serves, let him do so as by the
strength which God supplies; so that in all things
God may be glorified through Jesus Christ, to
whom belongs the glory and dominion forever
and ever. Amen (1 Pet. 4:7-11, NASB).

Why did our Lord teach us to pray "Thy kingdom come"? In the perception of those early disciples the coming of that kingdom meant the manifestation of the kingdom of Messiah. It was to be an open, public, and glorious manifestation on the earth. They were looking for the Lord's coming as they prayed, "Thy kingdom come." The blood-washed, Spirit-born church when rightly anticipating her Lord's return becomes exercised in intercessory prayer for the coming of the kingdom. In their assemblies, in their ordinance of communion, and in their prayer life, Christians are anticipating the coming of the Lord.

Fourth, the necessity of *preaching* was associated with the return of Christ. Paul charged Timothy:

I solemnly charge you in the presence of God and
of Christ Jesus, who is to judge the living and the
dead, and by His appearing and His kingdom:
preach the word; be ready in season and out of
season; reprove, rebuke, exhort, with great
patience and instruction (2 Tim. 4:1-2, NASB).

In His great Olivet discourse Christ made the preaching of the gospel a sign of the end. "And this gospel of the kingdom shall be preached in the whole world for a witness to all the nations, and then the end shall come" (Matt. 24:14, NASB). While waiting for Christ to return, the church does not remain passive. Pressed by the Holy Spirit, the church pours out its energies in aggressive world evangelism as a means of hastening the coming of the day of the Lord. The time segment between Christ's first coming and His Second Coming should be taken up with preaching the gospel to every creature.

A church that is waiting for Christ cannot be confined to ministry within the four walls of its own fellowship. It must break out and touch men everywhere. Both ministers and laymen must be motivated by the shortness of time and the expectation of Christ's Second Coming. The church does not have forever to do its work. Gospel preaching must be attended by a sense of urgency. The church must hasten with the news. Time is running out for world evangelism.

Finally, a careful search of the New Testament shows that the *praise* of the early church was also related to the coming of the Lord. Their acts of worship reflected an eschatological dimension. They worshiped the coming King.

> *Now to Him who is able to keep you from stumbling, and to make you stand in the presence of His glory blameless with great joy, to the only God our Savior, through Jesus Christ our Lord, be glory, majesty, dominion and authority, before all time and now and forever. Amen (Jude 24-25, NASB).*

The coming Christ is in the midst of His church now and He is to be adored and worshiped. The hope of His coming ought to saturate the praise of the waiting community.

How well would our churches fare in an evaluation

based on the assumption that the church should function as the community of saints who wait for their Lord's return? Does our assembly life reflect this biblical truth? Is our gathering at the Lord's table characterized by the glad anticipation of Christ's coming? Is the congregational prayer life indicative of a truly waiting community expecting the Son of God? Will the church meet the proclamation test? Is our praise full of the joy of His return?

The Christ who is coming is standing unseen in the church today. Did He not say that where two or three are gathered in His name, there He would be in the midst? John saw Him in the midst of the churches dressed in the garments of judgment (Rev. 1). He is evaluating the church in the light of her attitude toward His coming. Jesus gave the criteria for such an evaluation while He was still on earth:

> *"It is like a man, away on a journey, who upon leaving his house and putting his slaves in charge, assigning to each one his task, also commanded the doorkeeper to stay on the alert. Therefore, be on the alert—for you do not know when the master of the house is coming, whether in the evening, at midnight, at cockcrowing, or in the morning—lest he come suddenly and find you asleep. And what I say to you I say to all, 'Be on the alert!'" (Mark 13:34-37, NASB).*

Christ described the church as a household left in the charge of servants while the master is on a journey. The servants were given assignments in the light of the master's return. The time of the master's return was not made known. They were to conduct their work in such a manner as to be ready any time for his return. Today's Christians are the servants of this household and have been given the mandate to be faithful in view of Christ's imminent coming.

Is it possible that the servants of His household in this day have become so feverish with activity and so concerned with the gathering storm of world events that the hope of Christ's coming for them has been forgotten?

Jesus is coming for us and He is coming to put the lid on history. Jesus is coming to bring in the golden age, and to cover this old world with the glory of the Lord like the waters cover the sea! In view of the lateness of the hour, the church of God on earth should be on her feet with her head up and her heart beating with anticipation of the soon coming of her Lord.

The Effect on Individual Christian Behavior

Just as the doctrine of Christ's Second Coming marks every aspect of assembly life in the New Testament church, so it marks every aspect of behavior in the daily lives of individual Christians. This teaching is not a form of mysticism unrelated to the realities of life here and now. The hope of Christ's personal return is a practical belief that, when rightly understood, alters and moderates the way Christians live in this present world.

Since Christ may come at any time, the Christian ought to be ready, so as not to be taken by surprise. He should live in readiness for the coming of the Lord and anticipate that wonderful meeting with joy. Those who wait for Christ's return have a wholesome perspective on life. They develop attitudes of heart and mind that will fit them for this high point in their redemption—that is, their glorification. That translation will change our mortal bodies into immortal bodies.

Those who want to know God in fullness and to live triumphantly in this age of incredible evil, should constantly study the teachings of Christ and the apostles on the second advent, as recorded in Scripture. The breakdown among believers in living a consistent Christian life can be related to the neglect or the ignorance of what God has said in His Word about living in readiness for the coming of Christ. To be passive about this blessed hope contradicts every scriptural instruction on the subject. The hope of Christ's personal return to take His own—that where He is, there they may be—must be the daily consideration of every believer. We will look at two instances when Christ taught about the believer's readiness.

Christ was preaching one day on the appearing of the kingdom of God and, sensing that His audience was expecting the immediate appearance of the kingdom, He told them a parable to correct their misunderstanding.

> He said therefore, "A certain nobleman went to a distant country to receive a kingdom for himself, and then return. And he called ten of his slaves, and gave them ten minas, and said to them, 'Do business with this until I come back.' "But his citizens hated him, and sent a delegation after him, saying, 'We do not want this man to reign over us.' "And it came about that when he returned, after receiving the kingdom, he ordered that these slaves, to whom he had given the money, be called to him in order that he might know what business they had done. And the first appeared, saying, 'Master, your mina has made ten minas more.' "And he said to him, 'Well done, good slave, because you have been faithful in a very little thing, be in authority over ten cities.' "And the second came, saying, 'Your mina, master, has made five minas.' "And he said to him also, 'And you are to be over five cities.' "And another came, saying, 'Master, behold your mina, which I kept put away in a handkerchief; for I

was afraid of you, because you are an exacting man; you take up what you did not lay down, and reap what you did not sow.' "He said to him, 'By your own words I will judge you, you worthless slave. Did you know that I am an exacting man, taking up what I did not lay down, and reaping what I did not sow? Then why did you not put the money in the bank, and having come, I would have collected it with interest?' "And he said to the bystanders, 'Take the mina away from him, and give it to the one who has the ten minas.' "And they said to him, 'Master, he has ten minas already.' "I tell you, that to everyone who has shall more be given, but from the one who does not have, even what he does have shall be taken away. But these enemies of mine, who did not want me to reign over them, bring them here, and slay them in my presence" (Luke 19:12-27, NASB).

The parable of the nobleman sets forth a future manifestation of the kingdom and instructs God's people regarding the interim until Christ's return. The manifestation of the kingdom must await the return of the king. The import of this parable is that the king's servants must occupy themselves with useful employment while they await that return. The believer has received from Christ gifts and deposits of divine grace that should be used for His glory. The nobleman in the parable said to his servants, after having given them each an amount of money, "Do business with this until I come back." The individual Christian is here exhorted to a sacred stewardship. In anticipation of the unannounced return of Christ, he should be doing business for Christ every day. The strongest possible motivation for good stewardship is the coming of Christ.

Another parable of our Lord teaches the importance of possessing true spirituality in the light of Christ's coming.

> "Then the kingdom of heaven will be comparable to ten virgins, who took their lamps, and went out to meet the bridegroom. And five of them were foolish, and five were prudent. For when the foolish took their lamps, they took no oil with them, but the prudent took oil in flasks along with their lamps. Now while the bridegroom was delaying, they all got drowsy and began to sleep. But at midnight there was a shout, 'Behold, the bridegroom! Come out to meet him.' Then all those virgins arose, and trimmed their lamps. And the foolish said to the prudent, 'Give us some of your oil, for our lamps are going out.' But the prudent answered, saying, 'No, there will not be enough for us and you too; go instead to the dealers and buy some for yourselves.' And while they were going away to make the purchase, the bridegroom came, and those who were ready went in with him to the wedding feast; and the door was shut. And later the other virgins also came, saying, 'Lord, lord, open up for us.' But he answered and said, 'Truly I say to you, I do not know you.' Be on the alert then, for you do not know the day nor the hour" (Matt. 25:1-13, NASB).

The virgins represent those who profess faith in Christ. The parable teaches that a real difference exists between those who profess faith in Christ and those who in reality possess new life in Christ. Every church member and every professor of religion ought to contemplate the parable of the ten virgins. Jesus taught clearly the danger of false profession in light of the imminent coming of Christ.

The apostles in their letters to the churches, wrote often of the relationship between the believer's life style and his expectation of Christ's return. Paul wrote:

> For the grace of God has appeared, bringing sal-
> vation to all men, instructing us to deny ungodli-
> ness and worldly desires and to live sensibly,
> righteously and godly in the present age, looking
> for the blessed hope and the appearing of the
> glory of our great God and Savior, Christ Jesus
> (Titus 2:11-13, NASB).

The believer whose hope is fixed on the coming of Jesus is called to a life that stands in radical contrast to the world about him. He is a sanctified nonconformist. Godliness becomes his hallmark. He has claimed the provision of Christ for victory over the world system and is thereby liberated from its bondage to live "sensibly, righteously, and godly." This life style focuses on the return of Christ. What practical daily benefits come to those who thus anticipate the blessed hope.

James, the brother of Christ and the first pastor of the Jerusalem church, wrote an exhortation to practice patience in the light of the coming of Jesus.

> Be patient, therefore, brethren, until the coming
> of the Lord. Behold, the farmer waits for the
> precious produce of the soil, being patient about
> it, until it gets the early and late rains. You too be
> patient; strengthen your hearts, for the coming of
> the Lord is at hand (James 5:7-8, NASB).

The social and political climate of the last days produces frustration and difficulty for the people of God. James warned both labor and management of impending trouble. He predicted the economic injustices that would come. James teaches that in these circumstances the waiting church is to bear the fruit of patience.

The Christian who understands the imminency of Christ's return should be considerate of others. "Let your forbearing spirit be known to all men. The Lord is near [The Lord is at hand]" (Phil. 4:5, NASB). If the admonitions of the New Testament are followed, the truth of the blessed hope will not produce wild-eyed fanatics but stable, loving, godly, and useful people. Fanaticism begins when the dogmas of eschatology are divorced from their spiritual implications.

The hope of the Lord's coming equips the believer to cope with life in the real world. He is not a detached visionary but a servant committed to glorifying his Master in word and deed while he awaits His return.

The waiting church should give itself to Bible study. Believers are urged to take heed to the prophetic word in particular. The doctrine of last things requires obedience as do all other true doctrines.

The apostle Peter in his second epistle wrote:

> For we did not follow cleverly devised tales when we made known to you the power and coming of our Lord Jesus Christ, but we were eyewitnesses of His majesty. For when He received honor and glory from God the Father, such an utterance as this was made to Him by the Majestic Glory, "This is My beloved Son with whom I am well-pleased"—and we ourselves heard this utterance made from heaven when we were with Him on the holy mountain. And so we have the prophetic word made more sure, to which you do well to pay attention as to a lamp

shining in a dark place, until the day dawns and the morning star arises in your hearts (2 Pet. 1:16-19, NASB).

Peter was an eyewitness of Christ's transfiguration and could speak firsthand of the glory of Christ to be manifested at His coming. But the apostle considered the written Scriptures of greater value than his own personal experience in determining the truth of Christ's coming again. He recommends the Scriptures as certain and authoritative in what they reveal about the day of Christ.

Peter describes the prophetic word as "a lamp shining in a dark place." This analogy shows the Word of God as giving the end-time Christians a proper perspective of things in a world under judgment. The world at its best is still a dark place. For the diligent soul who searches the prophetic word for instruction, consolation, and perspective there will be light. As he awaits the dawn of the day of Christ the daystar arises in his heart. The daystar appears just before dawn when the night is the darkest. The staying power of God's people in these perilous last days is this deep inner experience with the indwelling Christ. For it is Christ, the Coming One, who is the daystar.

The church, then, is a waiting community. Every facet of its assembly life ought to reflect its anticipation of Christ's Second Coming. Individual believers within that community are to live in readiness for His return. It is the hope of Christ's coming that affects their everyday lives.

What is that hope? Is it the dark and dreadful days of wrath, or does the church look for the dawning of eternity's morning? The New Testament repeatedly projects the imminent return of Jesus Christ as the hope for God's people.

The social, economic, and political disasters of the past half century have prompted some evangelicals to reconsider the doctrine of hope. The suffering of Third World Christians and those behind the Iron Curtain has been taken as evidence that the church's ancient hope of deliverance from the great tribulation is wrong. On the supposition that the present bleak conditions in the world indicate that the church will go through the tribulation, the theologians have altered their position accordingly. Some have gone so far as to redefine the end-time church as a survival operation rather than a militant force to be reckoned with. Manuals have been written to train believers in the practical art of surviving during tribulation days.

Does this approach measure up to the expectation of the blessed hope? Did not the early Christians suffer persecution, imprisonment, and martyrdom, and all the while maintain hope of Christ's coming?

The doctrine of Christ's coming for His own is meant to be a comforting truth, according to Scripture (1 Thess. 4:18). The believer can hardly be comforted with the prospect of suffering the awful acts of judgment described in the Book of Revelation. The believer does not look for impending judgment but the imminent coming of Christ. The church is to escape the dark hours of God's wrath. The great tribulation is divine judgment poured out on rebellious Israel and the unrepentant Gentile nations. The prophetic hope of the church of God is not the coming darkness of midnight, but the dawn of the day of Christ.

2

The Birth Pangs of a New Age

The waiting church of New Testament times had the teachings of Jesus and of the apostles and the writings of the Old Testament prophets from which to draw their doctrine of last things. Basic to their understanding of the last days was the sermon Jesus gave His disciples on the Mount of Olives. This message is contained in all three synoptic Gospels (Matt. 24; Mark 13; Luke 21).

The Olivet discourse was given in full view of the city of Jerusalem. The outline of Herod's building projects stood out against the horizon. The disciples were obviously impressed with the size and beauty of these structures. Jesus saw their preoccupation with Herod's buildings as an opportunity to teach them of the heavenly view of such earthly grandeur. He responded to their comments with the prophecy that not one stone will be left on top of another when God's judgment falls on Herod's splendid buildings.

Jesus had announced His Second Coming just before He and the disciples left the city for the Mount of Olives (Matt. 23:39). The disciples had hardly taken in that word when Jesus predicted the coming apocalyptic judgment on Jerusalem. They pressed Jesus for an explanation of these two events. How would they know when these things were about to transpire? What signs could be expected to alert them to Christ's coming and the end of this age?

Before we look at Jesus' answer to the disciples' questions in detail, let us take a moment to consider the purpose of signs.

The Purpose of Signs

Consideration of the signs of the end of the age is not an exercise in futile curiosity. Jesus urged contemplation of the signs to alert the souls of the faithful and to warn the souls of the unfaithful.

The interest the Pharisees expressed in signs, however, was little more than curiosity. When the Pharisees and Sadducees approached Jesus to ask for a sign from heaven, Jesus discerned their hypocrisy and rebuked them.

> "When it is evening, you say, 'It will be fair weather, for the sky is red.' And in the morning, 'There will be a storm today, for the sky is red and threatening.' Do you know how to discern the appearance of the sky, but cannot discern the signs of the times? An evil and adulterous generation seeks after a sign; and a sign will not be given it, except the sign of Jonah." And He left them, and went away (Matt. 16:2b-4, NASB).

Spiritual ignorance of the real issues blinded the Pharisees to the signs of the times.

The root idea of signs in both the Hebrew and Greek languages is to discern or to receive understanding. Signs are not to be used in an intriguing game of speculation but rather as a solid basis for instruction and understanding. Preoccupation with signs that does not produce radical change in the life is less than biblical. The immediate impact of understanding the signs of the times should be a deeper commitment to Jesus Christ and a greater degree of nonconformity to the world system. For the signs, rightly understood, enlighten God's people regarding the divine judgment on human wickedness and call His people to a separated walk.

To be rightly understood, the prophetic signs must be interpreted in relation to time. To reject all reference to time in the consideration of prophetic truth is untenable. God has fixed a day for the prophetic events relating to the Second Coming of Christ and the ushering in of His kingdom. While we are clearly told in Scripture that no man knows the day or the hour of His coming, we are to observe the signs of the times so as not to be taken unaware by His sudden return.

The signs must also be interpreted as being progressive. The events attendant to Christ's personal return and the culmination of this age will occur in a time sequence. From the days of the apostles until now, the church has had to interpret the signs of the times. A new age is coming in time and space history, according to the Scripture. The church is to anticipate this event and should be able to detect the signs that point to it.

Jesus warned the residents of Jerusalem that their doom had been sealed because they failed to discern the times. They missed the first advent of Christ. They lived through the day of this divine visitation without ever understanding what was transpiring in their midst. They watched the Lamb of God being offered up for the sins of the world and shrugged the whole matter off as the well-deserved death of a religious fanatic.

Do signs matter? Certainly they matter. Signs, by definition, draw attention to something beyond themselves. The prophetic signs are to draw the believer's attention to Christ and His intervention in the culmination of the world system.

Christ's Teachings on Prophetic Signs

The Olivet discourse brings together Christ's teachings on prophetic signs. This message gives signs for the church and signs for Israel. Although the questions the disciples asked the Lord (Matt. 24:3) failed to distinguish between the destruction of Jerusalem and Christ's Second Coming, our Lord's answer does make the necessary distinction. We will be using the record of this discourse as found in Matthew 24 as the basis of our study.

The first set of signs, in verses 4-14, are said to be the "beginning of birth pangs." The waiting community is to understand that when these signs are prevalent, they signal the beginning of the travail that will give birth to the new age. How long the labor will be is a secret known only to God. No indication is given as to the time which will elapse from the beginning of travail until the birth of the new age. These indications are given not for the purpose of identifying the time of each sign, but for keeping the saints from deception and promoting their readiness for the Lord's return. The believer who has a right perception of the signs will be better equipped to live and minister in the end time.

Jesus responded to the disciples' inquiry about the signs of the end with these words:

> "See to it that no one misleads you. 5. For many will come in My name, saying, 'I am the Christ,' and will mislead many. 6. And you will be hearing of wars and rumors of wars; see that you are not frightened, for those things must take place, but that is not yet the end. 7. For nation will rise against nation, and kingdom against kingdom, and in various places there will be famines and earthquakes. 8. But all these things are merely the beginning of birth pangs. 9. Then they will deliver you up to tribulation, and will kill you, and you will be hated by all nations on account of My name. 10. And at that time many will fall away and will betray one another and

29

hate one another. 11. And many false prophets will arise, and will mislead many. 12. And because lawlessness is increased, most people's love will grow cold. 13. But the one who endures to the end, it is he who shall be saved. 14. And this gospel of the kingdom shall be preached in the whole world for a witness to all the nations, and then the end shall come" (Matt. 24:4-14, NASB).

Those signs mentioned in verses 4-6 apply to the whole gospel age. The last days began with Christ's first coming (Heb. 1:2). There is a sense in which the entire Christian dispensation is a part of the end time. The false prophets, wars, and rumors of wars have been the trends of the past two thousand years.

In verse 7, these trends escalate and the birth pangs truly begin. War and international unrest reach an all-time high. World War I seems to have been such a watershed in history. Not only the increase in the number of wars but also the development of formidable military capabilities leave little doubt that the world now stands at the "beginning of birth pangs."

The signs go beyond unprecedented political, social, and military unrest to famine and natural catastrophes. The world food situation is the concern of thinking people everywhere. Africa and Asia have suffered widespread famine, and some authorities are concerned that unless precautions are taken global famine is possible in the not-too-distant future.

According to a UNESCO report published in 1978 the governments of the world no longer consider earthquakes as just natural events but as natural hazards. The report says:

Earthquakes, among the most serious of all disasters which can befall mankind, deeply involve the responsibility of public authorities. Owing to their diversity and the extent, the disasters caused by earthquakes are often such as to render the social group struck by them incapable of aiding themselves with their own resources, usually destroyed, diminished, or rendered inoperative. The suddenness of an earthquake and the stupefaction of the victims preclude the improvisation of relief more than in the case of any other kind of disaster. . . .[1]

The United States government now appropriates some $80 million a year for research in earthquake hazard. The twentieth century has seen a marked increase in the number of major earthquakes. Scientists have compiled a list of 126 major earthquakes dating from 1505 through 1903. From 1904 through 1974 a total of 114 major earthquakes occurred. The number of earthquakes since 1900 has climbed beyond the total of the previous four centuries.[2]

Beginning in verse 9, Jesus addresses the religious signs. The intense persecution of God's people will result in suffering and martyrdom for many Christians. This prediction takes on new meaning when we realize that more believers have been martyred during the twentieth century than at any other time in the Christian era.

Apostasy and false religions will abound in the last days. The Protestant churches and the Roman church have already suffered the inroads of theological liberalism to such an extent that the voice of the church in the so-called Christian nations has almost been stilled. The culture of Western nations is near collapse as a result of the forsaking of the moral and ethical concepts of the Christian system.

The details of the spiritual confusion Jesus predicted would come in the last days are amplified in the New Testament epistles. The apostle Paul said:

> But the Spirit explicitly says that in later times some will fall away from the faith, paying attention to deceitful spirits and doctrines of demons, by means of the hypocrisy of liars seared in their own conscience as with a branding iron, men who forbid marriage and advocate abstaining from foods, which God has created to be gratefully shared in by those who believe and know the truth (1 Tim. 4:1-3, NASB).

The increase of apostasy and heretical doctrine is a portent of the end time.

One bright light shines against the darkness of social unrest, war, famine, natural disaster, and the collapse of civilization, and that is the persistent preaching of the gospel. Jesus said, "And this gospel of the kingdom shall be preached in the whole world for a witness to all the nations, and then the end shall come" (v. 14). Some Bible scholars have applied this verse to the Jewish witness during the tribulation period, contending that the gospel of the kingdom is not the same gospel as that preached by the church. The difficulty with that interpretation is the biblical declaration that there is only one gospel (Gal. 1:6-9). The kingdom of God in all its aspects is a part of the message of the gospel. Wherever the gospel is preached in the world, the truth both of Christ's first coming and of His Second Coming must be a part of that proclamation. World evangelism is to continue until Christ comes. Jesus reassured the disciples of this fact before His ascension.

> "Go therefore and make disciples of all the

nations, baptizing them in the name of the Father
and the Son and the Holy Spirit, teaching them to
observe all that I commanded you; and lo, I am
with you always, even to the end of the age"
(Matt. 28:19-20, NASB).

The experience of the church confirms Christ's words. In
spite of every force of wickedness and the incredible
confusion in the international scene, the process of world
evangelism continues. The signs of the times when rightly
comprehended encourage the all-out effort of the church to
reach the world with the gospel.

In the second set of signs, verses 15-28, the scope is
narrowed to a smaller time frame. Jesus spoke of an event
rather than a trend.

"Therefore when you see the abomination of
desolation which was spoken of through Daniel
the prophet, standing in the holy place (let the
reader understand), 16. then let those who are in
Judea flee to the mountains; 17. let him who is on
the housetop not go down to get the things out
that are in his house; 18. and let him who is in the
field not turn back to get his cloak. 19. But woe to
those who are with child and to those who nurse
babes in those days! 20. But pray that your flight
may not be in the winter, or on a Sabbath; 21. for
then there will be a great tribulation, such as has
not occurred since the beginning of the world
until now, nor ever shall. 22. And unless those
days had been cut short, no life would have been
saved; but for the sake of the elect those days
shall be cut short. 23. Then if any one says to you,
'Behold, here is the Christ,' or 'There He is,' do not
believe him. 24. For false Christs and false

> prophets will arise and will show great signs and wonders, so as to mislead, if possible, even the elect. 25. Behold, I have told you in advance. 26. If therefore they say to you, 'Behold, He is in the wilderness,' do not go forth, or, 'Behold, He is in the inner rooms,' do not believe them. 27. For just as the lightning comes from the east, and flashes even to the west, so shall the coming of the Son of Man be. 28. Wherever the corpse is, there the vultures will gather" (Matt. 24:15-28, NASB).

Referring the disciples to Daniel's prophecy, Jesus warned of the coming danger of the very last days. The labor pains will be intense. This passage gives some of the identifying signs of the tribulation period. From the antichrist's abominable act in the temple, as predicted by Daniel, until the public appearing of Christ will be a dark and fearful time.

Jesus suggested that the key to understanding the period He was about to describe is a reference in the Book of Daniel. Gabriel appeared to Daniel and instructed him:

> "And he will make a firm covenant with the many for one week, but in the middle of the week he will put a stop to sacrifice and grain offering; and on the wing of abominations will come one who makes desolate, even until a complete destruction, one that is decreed, is poured out on the one who makes desolate" (Dan. 9:27, NASB).

The open manifestation of the antichrist by his desecration of the temple will signal the beginning of the darkest days in human history. Since the center of this awful atrocity will be the city of Jerusalem, the residents of Judea who are believers are warned to flee in that hour. While this passage has ministered comfort and instruction to persecuted believers throughout the history of the church, it seems to have a specific application to the saints of the great tribulation.

The final set of signs, verses 29-31, describes the coming of Christ.

> "But immediately after the tribulation of those days the sun will be darkened, and the moon will not give its light, and the stars will fall from the sky, and the powers of the heavens will be shaken, 30. and then the sign of the Son of Man will appear in the sky, and then all the tribes of the earth will mourn, and they will see the Son of Man coming on the clouds of the sky with power and great glory. 31. And He will send forth His angels with a great trumpet and they will gather together His elect from the four winds, from one end of the sky to the other" (Matt. 24:29-31, NASB).

Christ's advent is said to come immediately after the short period called the great tribulation. His coming will be attended by many signs and wonders in the heavens. The greatest sign is called the "sign of the Son of Man." This may speak of the appearance of Christ with the armies of heaven as described in Revelation 19. Then, in verse 31, the angels will gather the Jews and Gentiles that have come to know Christ during the tribulation days. This verse 32 is not referring to the rapture of the church, for Christ himself will come to take His church (1 Thess. 4:16). Here the circumstances are different in that angels are sent to gather the elect; the elect in this verse are the tribulation saints mentioned in verse 22.

Having answered the disciples' questions about the

signs of the end of the age, Jesus then applied the truth of the signs of His coming in verses 32-51. The waiting community is urged to watchfulness.

> *"For this reason you be ready too; for the Son of Man is coming at an hour when you do not think He will"* (Matt. 24:44, NASB).

Christ's application is for us today. The signs are true indicators of the nearness of the termination of this age and the birth of a new age—the literal kingdom of Christ—and thus should be taken seriously by the followers of Christ. Although Christ answered His disciples regarding the entire sequence of eschatological events, He stressed the importance His coming has to His waiting people.

Unfortunately, some evangelicals have become more interested in predicting the time of events than in the significance of Christ's return for them personally. The efforts of some Bible teachers to pinpoint every prophetic event and to predict the actual time of Christ's coming have been spiritually devastating to the church. However, overreaction to this error has led many into the equal error of denying any time factors in relationship to Christ's return, thus altering the teaching on Christ's return from a literal event to a spiritual principle.

Between these two extremes can be found a sane and scriptural approach to the time frame of eschatology. A basic law of interpretation is that the plain literal sense of a passage should be accepted unless the form or context indicates otherwise. There is a prophetic time frame. Certain events—such as the gathering of the church, the great tribulation, the appearance and reign of the antichrist, the public appearance of Christ, the judgment of the nations, the spiritual restoration of Israel, the manifestation of the kingdom of heaven, the great white throne judgment—are predicted in the Scriptures. These are not spiritual principles but literal events destined to occur in time and space history. In fact, the Scriptures even give the actual duration of some prophetic events. Therefore, how the events of prophecy interrelate should be of concern to the student of the Bible. Otherwise, are we to believe that so much detail is to have no particular meaning to the believer? To deny the time frame of prophecy is either to lock in mystery large portions of the Scripture or to spiritualize the meaning.

However, to be so concerned with the details to the neglect of desire for Christ's return for us personally is equally in error. The New Testament speaks so often of the return of Christ that it seems to overshadow many other themes. The earliest creeds of Christendom affirm the church's faith in the personal return of the Lord Jesus Christ. As the purpose of His first advent was redemptive, so is the purpose of His second advent. The tendency to consider Christ's return as an event among many events which make up the last days can blind us to the more refined redemptive reasons for His coming. Let us give heed to the heart of Bible prophecy. Jesus may come at any time to put the finishing touches on our salvation. Can we join with John in saying "Even so, come quickly, Lord Jesus"?

---

1. Jean Douarel, "Social and Administrative Implications, Protection, Relief, Rehabilitation" in *The Assessment and Mitigation of Earthquake Risk*, UNESCO, 1978, p. 286.

2. G. A. Eiby, *All about Earthquakes* (New York: Harper & Row Pub., 1957), pp. 153-159.

3

The Rapture of the Church

From the divine perspective there have been only a few important happenings in the world since Adam was expelled from the Garden of Eden. A baby was born in Bethlehem whose name was Jesus. Jesus grew to manhood and when He was thirty years of age John the Baptist baptized Him in the Jordan River. The Holy Spirit led Him into the wilderness where He was tested forty days. Jesus returned from the wilderness and in the power of the Spirit of God began to preach the gospel. For three and a half years He ministered with great power. Jesus' enemies sent Him to Calvary where He was crucified. His body was laid in the tomb, but the tomb could not hold Him. On the third day He came forth from the grave. For forty days He remained on earth and then ascended into heaven from Mount Olivet. The disciples returned to Jerusalem and waited ten days in the upper room until the Holy Spirit came. The incarnation of Christ, His death, His resurrection, and the coming of the Spirit constitute the high points of redemptive history.

The next great redemptive happening will be the Second Coming of the Lord Jesus Christ. The same Jesus who came to earth in history past is coming a second time. The return of Christ is not just a single event, but a panorama of events. It can be compared to a dramatic production with many scenes. Before discussing these scenes in detail, we need to have an overview of this great drama of the return of the Son of God to this earth.

In one of the scenes of this great drama, the Scriptures teach that Jesus will restore Israel in fulfillment of the promises God gave to Abraham, Isaac, and Jacob. Our Lord will also deal with the Gentile nations of this world. The nations of this earth that have for so long rejected His laws of righteousness will be confronted by the Son of God in all His glory. In the end of this age there shall emerge several important leaders with influence on the events of the world. Among these will be the antichrist. When Jesus returns, He will defeat the antichrist and bring his forces to an end. Christ will openly and publicly deal with Satan and all His spiritual enemies. Then He will establish His kingdom right here in time and space. This millennial reign will be followed by the final judgment. Beyond the scene of the great white throne judgment lie the new heavens and the new earth. Finally, the appearance of the new heavens and new earth signifies the eternal age.

Before any of these scenes are enacted, however, Christ is coming first to rapture His church. Little is said about this aspect of Christ's return in the Old Testament. Though the Second Coming is very plain in the Old Testament, the fact of Christ's coming for His church is kept in mystery form. The Old Testament does illustrate this truth in some of its types. Two men, Enoch and Elijah, were translated without dying. Daniel speaks of a coming resurrection of the righteous to everlasting life. So the rapture was implied, but not clearly explained.

In His public discourses Jesus had much to say about His Second Coming and the signs of the times announcing that event. As we saw in the previous chapter, the sermon Christ preached on the Mount of Olives gives a broad view of end-time events. Jesus enunciated the political, social, and spiritual situation on earth during the last days. He spoke of Israel and of the nations of the world at the end of the age. But in the Gospel of John, Jesus gives a distinctly different perspective on His coming. He says nothing about Israel or the judgment or the signs of the times. There are only three references to the Second Coming of Christ in the whole Gospel of John, and all three relate to His coming for the church.

Jesus' Teachings on the Rapture

In the upper room the night before Jesus went to the cross, He gave His last words of instruction to His disciples:

> "Let not your heart be troubled; believe in God, believe also in Me. In My Father's house are many dwelling places; if it were not so, I would have told you; for I go to prepare a place for you. And if I go and prepare a place for you, I will come again, and receive you to Myself; that where I am, there you may be also" (John 14:1-3, NASB).

That night Jesus unfolded a great mystery that had been in the heart of God since before the world was made—the rapture of the church. He promised that He would come in person to take the church off the earth's scene. He said "I will come again, and receive you to Myself." He did not give the details of that event, for the disciples were not ready for it. Instead, He told them,

> "I have many more things to say to you, but you cannot bear them now. But when He, the Spirit of truth, comes, He will guide you into all the truth; . . .He will disclose to you what is to come" (John 16:12-13, NASB).

After Jesus ascended, He sent the Holy Spirit to His church. The Holy Spirit inspired the apostles to write the truth He revealed concerning the Second Coming of the

Lord and especially about His coming for the church.

Paul's Teachings on the Rapture

The apostle Paul received a revelation describing the manner in which the Lord will come for His people.

> But we do not want you to be uninformed, breth-
> ren, about those who are asleep, that you may not
> grieve, as do the rest who have no hope. For if we
> believe that Jesus died and rose again, even so
> God will bring with Him those who have fallen
> asleep in Jesus. For this we say to you by the
> word of the Lord, that we who are alive, and
> remain until the coming of the Lord, shall not pre-
> cede those who have fallen asleep. For the Lord
> Himself will descend from heaven with a shout,
> with the voice of the archangel, and with the
> trumpet of God; and the dead in Christ shall rise
> first. Then we who are alive and remain shall be
> caught up together with them in the clouds to
> meet the Lord in the air, and thus we shall always
> be with the Lord. Therefore comfort one another
> with these words (1 Thess. 4:13-18, NASB).

This passage gives an explicit explanation of Christ's coming to take His people from the earth's scene. Before we look at the context in which Paul was writing, note the implication of this passage. There is an essential distinction between Christ's coming for the church and His appearance to establish the millennial kingdom. The coming of the Lord Jesus for His people is imminent; that is simply, it could happen at any time. There are no signs to be fulfilled before Jesus comes to receive His own.

The import of imminency was illustrated for me by an

experience I had while returning from Europe on a KLM 747. As we were drawing near to New York City, the voice of the pilot came over the loudspeaker saying, "Our approach to Kennedy Airport is imminent." I thought, "My, what an interesting way to put it. Will anybody understand him?" Everybody understood him. People went into action all over that plane. Some were getting their packages together, and the men were straightening up their ties. All began to ready themselves for landing. They knew what imminent meant. It meant that any minute now the plane would be in New York. The imminence of the coming of Christ means that at any minute now the Lord may come!

Some Bible students find difficulty with the fact that Paul throughout his ministry believed in the imminent coming of the Lord, but Christ did not return during Paul's lifetime. Since the days of the apostle, many enlightened saints have lived in the same expectation of the momentary coming of the Lord. The critics maintain that since the Lord has not returned, those people were mistaken in their judgment. No, they were not mistaken; they understood the Bible. The apostles taught that Christ could come at any time and that all believers should live in readiness for His appearing.

There is a difference also between Christ's coming for His people and Christ's coming with His people. Zechariah 14 describes a scene in which Christ comes down to the earth. The Mount of Olives is designated as the very spot on earth where His feet will touch. The prophetic scene in Zechariah 14:1-9 applies to Christ's coming with His people. When Jesus comes for His church, He will not descend to the earth but will come in the air. His descent into the air will be attended by a shout, the voice of an archangel, and the sound of the trumpet. The word translated "shout" is the word of command, a signal for action. It is a military term that an officer would use when ordering his men into battle. When our Lord descends into the air, He will give a great battle cry that will awaken all the dead saints out of their graves and transform all the living saints and gather His army to meet Him in the sky. This same army will come back with Him out of the glory world when Jesus reigns as King of Kings.

In this passage in Thessalonians, then, Paul is describing the first happening of the Lord's return—the rapture of the church. What was the occasion for Paul's teaching? Paul wrote to the church at Thessalonica to answer some questions on the doctrine of the Second Coming. As the founder of that church, he had taught them all they knew. Unfortunately, some of them had misunderstood the prophetic Scriptures and they thought the Lord had already come and were concerned that they were left behind. They pondered the fate of the righteous dead. So the first question this passage addresses is, What will happen to those who have fallen asleep in Jesus?

Paul told the Thessalonians not to be concerned about the believers who are asleep, for they will be awakened when Christ comes. This analogy to sleep depicts death not as a horrifying experience, but as a beautiful entrance into rest. Some teachers draw from Paul's use of the word sleep a doctrine called soul sleeping. They teach that when one dies he enters a state of sleep that is prolonged until the resurrection. The concept of soul sleeping is a misinterpretation of Paul's use of the word *sleep*. Sleep is only an analogy of death indicating the peacefulness of the death of the righteous. The body rests in the grave, but the saint of God is in the bosom of Jesus. Paul also wrote that to be absent from the body is to be present with the Lord (2 Cor. 5:8). Those who die in Christ are immediately in the conscious presence of the Lord. The righteous dead enjoy the blessings of divine presence while they anticipate the glad hour of the resurrection when their soul, spirit, and body will again be joined together.

What a dramatic scene will take place when Jesus comes. The cemeteries will be quaking as saints long dead are resurrected. Bodies in the bottom of the sea and at the bottom of lakes and rivers will be instantaneously resurrected in a recognizable form. No matter how mutilated the body may have been or how many centuries the body may have been dead, Christ will raise it up.

Paul speaks of this resurrection as the redemption of the body, a full adoption into sonship.

> And not only this, but also we ourselves, having the first fruits of the Spirit, even we ourselves groan within ourselves, waiting eagerly for our adoption as sons, the redemption of our body (Rom. 8:23, NASB).

The Book of Revelation describes the rapture as the first resurrection. (The Bible teaches more than one resurrection.)

> And I saw thrones, and they sat upon them, and judgment was given to them. And I saw the souls of those who had been beheaded because of the testimony of Jesus and because of the word of God, and those who had not worshiped the beast or his image, and had not received the mark upon their forehead and upon their hand; and **they came to life** (emphasis added) and reigned with Christ for a thousand years (Rev. 20:4, NASB).

The Greek word translated "came to life" is translated "resurrection" in five other New Testament passages. Verses 5 and 6 say:

The rest of the dead did not come to life until the thousand years were completed. This is the first resurrection. Blessed and holy is the one who has a part in the first resurrection; over these the second death has no power, but they will be priests of God and of Christ and will reign with Him for a thousand years.

There is widespread interest today in the subject of death. The broadcast media and magazine publications have picked up this theme. The publishing industry is doing its share to feed the market with books on death. Sociologists are trying to explain it, medicine is trying to define it, science is trying to analyze it. All to no avail. Their failure is the direct result of a humanistic approach to the subject of death. All the combined efforts of these disciplines of learning will not find a proper answer for death. The only viable explanation of death is found in the Word of God. Christ rose from the dead and has broken death's power. He took the sting out of death. He is alive forevermore. By His power He will make all things new. To be a Christian is to have the same Spirit in us that raised the Son of God from the dead. Our hope is to be raised from the dead!

Christians need not sorrow like others who have no hope. The Christian's hope is in the Second Coming of the Lord Jesus Christ at which time He will resurrect the righteous and translate the living believers.

Having answered the Thessalonians' concern about the righteous dead, Paul went on to answer a second question, What will happen to the living Christians when Christ comes? Paul says, "Then we who are alive and remain shall be caught up together with them in the clouds to meet the Lord in the air." Paul wrote the same explanation to the Corinthians:

> Behold, I tell you a mystery; we shall not all
> sleep, but we shall all be changed, in a moment, in
> the twinkling of an eye, at the last trumpet; for
> the trumpet will sound, and the dead will be
> raised imperishable, and we shall be changed (1
> Cor. 15:51-52, NASB).

Not every Christian will die. There will be a generation of
Christians that will not die—those that are alive when the
Lord comes. They will be instantaneously changed by the
supernatural power of God. The resurrection life of Jesus
Christ will come into them and transform their bodies.

The Greek verb translated "caught up" means "to
seize" or "to snatch." It implies that something is taken with
irresistible force and moved rapidly to another location.
When Christ comes into the air, the mighty force of the
Spirit of God will snatch every Christian up to meet the
Lord in the air. God's work in the rapture is surely a
contrast to human endeavors to place men in space! The
U.S. government has spent billions of dollars to probe the
mysteries of space. Scientists have learned enough to hurl a
man through space to the moon and bring him back again.
Elaborate and expensive equipment is needed for man to
travel in space. The redeemed will have no need of such
space equipment. When Christ comes, He will give us new
bodies with dimensions capable of going through space and
anywhere God wants us to go in His universe. And 1 Corinthians 15 speaks to the speed with which the rapture will
take place. As quickly as you can blink your eye, the church
will be caught up to meet the Lord in the air.

The living believers, together with the resurrected
saints, will be elevated to meet the Lord in the air. Both the
dead and the living Christians share this blessed hope. If
the Lord should come at this moment, every Christian's
body would be immediately translated into its resurrection

form—incorruptible, immortal, never to die again.

In his letter to the Philippians, Paul describes the effects of the rapture:

> For our citizenship is in heaven, from which also we eagerly wait for a Savior, the Lord Jesus Christ; who will transform the body of our humble state into conformity with the body of His glory, by the exertion of the power that He has even to subject all things to Himself (Phil. 3:20-21, NASB).

Translation will make our bodies conformable to the body of the Lord Jesus Christ.

The Final Stage of Our Salvation

The coming of the Lord for us constitutes the final stage of our salvation. Biblical salvation is composed of justification, regeneration, sanctification, glorification. Justification takes place when we believe. In the courts of heaven our record is cleared on the basis of the shed blood of Jesus Christ—a full satisfaction of our sins has been made and God acquits us. Because of the imposition of the blood of the Lamb, we stand before Him justified as though we had never sinned. While justification transpires in heaven, another miracle goes on in the believer's heart—he is regenerated and brought to life spiritually. Sanctification is that aspect of biblical salvation that matures the character of the child of God. It is initiated by the infilling of the Holy Spirit. From that point the believer can begin to grow in grace and in the knowledge of the Lord Jesus Christ. Sanctification requires full consecration of one's self to God. This spiritual crisis into the sanctified life leads to an ever-expanding life of blessing.

But after we are saved and sanctified, there remains another aspect of biblical salvation that has yet to be completed—our glorification. The mortal body is within the grasp of death because of sin. But in the final stage of our salvation, our bodies will be freed forever from the ravages of sin and death. The body is not inherently wicked. The Bible declares the body to be a creation of God. It is just as sacred to the Almighty as the soul and the spirit. Therefore the plan of salvation saves the whole man, not part of him. God's plan is to make the sinner whole in spirit, soul, and body. Even now the blessing of healing is a foretaste of the resurrection. We read in Romans 8:11:

> But if the Spirit of Him who raised Jesus from the dead dwells in you, He who raised Christ Jesus from the dead will also give life to your mortal bodies through His Spirit who indwells you (NASB).

The same life that will one day raise this body up for its final healing and deliverance from death is the very same power that brings healing to us now.

The resurrection of the dead saints and the translation of the living saints is the final stage of our salvation. Instantaneously we will be forever freed of all our limitations. The weaknesses and infirmities that plague us now will be gone. The physical weaknesses, the personality weaknesses, and the spiritual weaknesses will be replaced by His strength. Glorification will perfectly fit us to serve Jesus Christ for all eternity.

How the believer's heart thrills at the thought of that wonderful day, when the church is called into the presence of the Lord. What a fellowship, what a reunion that will be! The Christian's hope is not the vain imagination of an over-worked religious zeal. It is the word of truth revealed by

God. The God of ultimate authority has spoken, and as surely as the sun comes up in the morning and sets in the evening, everything God has said in the Bible will be fulfilled completely.

Christ is the central attraction at the meeting in the air. The church is gathered to meet Him. The apostle John brought this truth into focus when he wrote:

> See how great a love the Father has bestowed upon us, that we should be called children of God; and such we are. For this reason the world does not know us, because it did not know Him. Beloved, now we are children of God, and it has not appeared as yet what we shall be. We know that, when He appears, we shall be like Him, because we shall see Him just as He is. And every one who has this hope fixed on Him purifies himself, just as He is pure (1 John 3:1-3, NASB).

John understood the hope of the Lord's coming to be a purifying hope. It compels believers to evaluate everything in their lives in the light of Christ's return. The rapture will be a face-to-face meeting with Christ after having followed without seeing Him, except with the eyes of faith. Believers now, like Moses of old, endure "as seeing Him who is unseen [invisible]" (Heb. 11:27, NASB). God's people are walking by faith now, but the day is coming when faith will turn to sight. When the Lord summons us to meet Him in the air, we will see Jesus! We will look upon His face. It staggers the mind to contemplate the privilege of this glorious exchange with Christ. In those sacred moments we should be able to look at the wounds in His hands and the scars on His brow and to thank Him for Calvary. From that moment on, we shall *always* be with the Lord. No more separation, no veil between. The rapture will accomplish in each believer such a total glorification as to fit him for the immediate presence of Christ and the indescribable blessing of everlasting life.

The interim between the rapture and the return of Christ with His church will be taken up in a series of important events. During the interval the believers will appear before the judgment seat of Christ. The purpose of judgment will not be to determine their salvation, but to determine their rewards on the basis of their works (2 Cor. 5:10; Rom. 14:10; 2 Tim. 4:8).

From the judgment seat of Christ the raptured saints will be ushered into the Marriage Supper of the Lamb. They will at last know the full reality of that which all their love feasts on earth were but a mere shadow. Dressed in righteousness, the church saints will be seated as the Bride of Christ.

4

The Great Tribulation

Church history offers abundant evidence that the community of faith is not immune from suffering. The tribulations of God's people take up much of the historical narrative of Scripture. Both the Old and New Testaments teach believers how to live in times of tribulation and suffering. No one can study the Word without discovering a theology of suffering. The Bible asserts that suffering will be the common experience of those who trust the Lord and identify with His name.

The patriarchs knew trials in their pilgrimages. The prophets were often under great pressure and at times suffered violence and even martyrdom. The kings who reigned in Jerusalem saw sorrow and suffering, both personal and national. Israel as a nation tasted the tribulation worked by evil nations against them as God's covenant people.

The early church experienced a baptism of fire that lasted for more than a century throughout the Roman Empire. Christianity was considered a threat to the Romans' doctrine of emperor worship. Persecuted and driven underground, the suffering church prevailed over every obstacle.

What era of church history can we read that does not tell of tribulation for the people of God? Leading up to and following the Reformation, the true believers of the Scriptures often were persecuted. The Waldensians and the Huguenots were persecuted unmercifully by the Roman church. The Anabaptists of Germany and Switzerland suffered incredible tribulation during the early days of the

Reformation. The English church suppressed the Puritans within their ranks, causing them deep suffering. The great John Bunyan, author of *The Pilgrim's Progress*, spent long years in prison as a result of his beliefs regarding the church. Many of the immigrants to America in colonial times were religious refugees fleeing persecution by the state churches of Europe.

The twentieth century exceeds all other centuries in the extent of suffering by the church. More martyrs have given their lives for the sake of Christ since 1900 than in any other century since Pentecost. Bible-believing Christians in Europe and Asia have suffered and in many places are continuing to suffer a blood bath as the Communist regimes of both Russia and China unleash their hatred for the church of God. Christians in general and leaders in particular have been imprisoned and often put to death because they would not renounce the gospel of Christ. Believers in the countries of Southeast Asia are now experiencing the same repression and persecution. Untold numbers of Christians were slaughtered in Cambodia under the Pol Pot government. The church in Viet Nam is slowly being restrained, and its leaders are suffering indignities and threats. The church in Laos is no exception to such tribulation.

Even in countries of peace and affluence the people of God know suffering. Those who stand for the perspective of Scripture and call for a renewal of righteousness in the culture feel the sting of retaliation from a self-indulgent society. It is not easy to be a Christian in our times. It has never been easy to be a Christian. A part of the Christian's calling is to suffer for Christ.

The Holy Spirit revealed to the apostle Paul that the last days would be dangerous for Christians.

But realize this, that in the last days difficult

times will come. For men will be lovers of self, lovers of money, boastful, arrogant, revilers, disobedient to parents, ungrateful, unholy, unloving, irreconcilable, malicious gossips, without self-control, brutal, haters of good, treacherous, reckless, conceited, lovers of pleasure rather than lovers of God; holding to a form of godliness, although they have denied its power; and avoid such men as these. For among them are those who enter into households and captivate weak women weighted down with sins, led on by various impulses, always learning and never able to come to the knowledge of the truth. And just as Jannes and Jambres opposed Moses, so these men also oppose the truth, men of depraved mind, rejected as regards the faith. But they will not make further progress; for their folly will be obvious to all, as also that of those two came to be. But you followed my teaching, conduct, purpose, faith, patience, love, perseverance, persecutions, sufferings, such as happened to me at Antioch, at Iconium and at Lystra; what persecutions I endured, and out of them all the Lord delivered me! And indeed, all who desire to live godly in Christ Jesus will be persecuted (2 Tim. 3:1-12, NASB).

The "last days" of which Paul wrote began at the first coming of Christ. Difficult times have characterized the church age. We are now in the last days of the last days. Persecution, suffering, and tribulation have been the lot of the church over these past two millenniums. The extent and intensity of these conditions in the world has escalated the level of persecution in the past few decades.

Christians need to be instructed in the New Testament teachings on suffering and God's rich provision for delivering His people in the midst of persecution. End-time Christians are already experiencing the stepped-up activities of the workers of darkness to thwart the witness of the church. The church is the last light left burning in this dark world and Satan will use every effort to put out that flame. Informed Christians know how to stand firm in difficult times. The grace and power of Christ implanted by the Holy Spirit sustain the child of God even through martyrdom.

The Church and the Great Tribulation

Because of the prevailing condition of tribulation across the centuries, some have concluded that the church will go through the great tribulation as well. The defenders of this position point to the history of the suffering church to support their conclusion that the church will be left on earth during that prophetic period. They further claim that to remove the church before the great tribulation would promote a weak kind of escapism for Christians. Nothing could be farther from the truth. No careful student of Scripture can find support for any theory that immunizes the church from suffering. It will be a suffering church that is caught up to meet Jesus in the air. Many will be raptured from concentration camps, prisons, and ghettos when Christ comes for His own. Some saints will be emaciated, hungry, and psychologically weary from tribulation.

The problem arises from the failure to differentiate between tribulation in general and *the great tribulation.* The prophetic Scriptures speak of a distinct block of time known as the great tribulation. This great tribulation is not the same as the troubles that have attended the church throughout her history. It is not the same as the difficult times now upon the world and called by Jesus, "the beginning of sorrows" (Matt. 24:8, KJV). Like a pregnant woman's first birth pain, they announce a far more intense time of difficulty than the world has previously known.

The great tribulation is a definite time period. It has a beginning and an end. The duration of this period of trouble is prescribed by the Word of God. The great tribulation is not an aggregate term for all the tribulation of the ages but refers to a specific time of tribulation.

> "Therefore when you see the abomination of desolation which was spoken of through Daniel the prophet, standing in the holy place (let the reader understand), then let those who are in Judea flee to the mountains; let him who is on the housetop not go down to get the things out that are in his house; and let him who is in the field not turn back to get his cloak. But woe to those who are with child and to those who nurse babes in those days! But pray that your flight may not be in the winter, or on a Sabbath; for then there will be a great tribulation, such as has not occurred since the beginning of the world until now, nor ever shall. And unless those days had been cut short, no life would have been saved; but for the sake of the elect those days shall be cut short" (Matt. 24:15-22, NASB).

This period of tribulation is distinguished by its intensity. It has, according to the words of Christ, no counterpart either in the history that precedes it or in the history that follows it. The great tribulation is a unique prophetic event. The intensity of this period is so great that it must of necessity be kept short to prevent the annihilation of the human race.

Israel and the Great Tribulation

The Jewish nation will suffer much during the great tribulation. The Old Testament prophets foresaw the advent of this season of suffering for the Jews. Moses was the first to predict this tribulation:

> "When you are in distress and all these things have come upon you, in the latter days, you will return to the Lord your God and listen to His voice" (Deut. 4:30, NASB).

The prophet continues his discourse by saying that this time of Jacob's trouble will be followed by the restoration of the nation (Jer. 30:9, 10).

During the exile Daniel spoke of the coming tribulation of Israel. The onset of the great tribulation period is described in the Book of Daniel:

> "Seventy weeks have been decreed for your people and your holy city, to finish the transgression, to make an end of sin, to make atonement for iniquity, to bring in everlasting righteousness, to seal up vision and prophecy, and to anoint the most holy place. So you are to know and discern that from the issuing of a decree to restore and rebuild Jerusalem until Messiah the Prince there will be seven weeks and sixty-two weeks; it will be built again, with plaza and moat, even in times of distress. Then after the sixty-two weeks the Messiah will be cut off and have nothing, and the people of the prince who is to come will destroy the city and the sanctuary. And its end will come with a flood; even to the end there will be war; desolations are

determined. And he will make a firm covenant
with the many for one week, but in the middle of
the week he will put a stop to sacrifice and grain
offering; and on the wing of abominations will
come one who makes desolate, even until a complete destruction, one that is decreed, is poured
out on the one who makes desolate" (Dan. 9:24-
27, NASB).

The first sixty-nine weeks of years have already tran-
spired in Hebrew history and brought the nation up to the
time of Christ. The seventieth week remains to be fulfilled.

Later in the book Daniel adds the detail of intensity to
his prophecy:

"Now at that time Michael, the great prince who
stands guard over the sons of your people, will
arise. And there will be a time of distress such as
never occurred since there was a nation until that
time; and at that time your people, everyone who
is found written in the book will be rescued"
(Dan. 12:1, 2, NASB).

Another prophet from Israel's exile predicted the great
distress to come upon the Jews in the end time:

"And I shall bring you out from the peoples and
gather you from the lands where you are
scattered, with a mighty hand and with an out-
stretched arm and with wrath poured out; and I
shall bring you into the wilderness of the
peoples, and there I shall enter into judgment
with you face to face. As I entered into judgment
with your fathers in the wilderness of the land of
Egypt, so I will enter into judgment with you,"

declares the Lord God. "And I shall make you pass under the rod, and I shall bring you into the bond of the covenant; and I shall purge from you the rebels and those who transgress against Me; I shall bring them out of the land where they sojourn, but they will not enter the land of Israel. Thus you will know that I am the Lord" (Ezek. 20:34-38, NASB).

God will mete out judgment on Israel during the dark days of the tribulation.

And the word of the Lord came to me saying, "Son of man, the house of Israel has become dross to Me; all of them are bronze and tin and iron and lead in the furnace; they are the dross of silver. Therefore, thus says the Lord God, 'Because all of you have become dross, therefore, behold, I am going to gather you into the midst of Jerusalem. As they gather silver and bronze and iron and lead and tin into the furnace to blow fire on it in order to melt it, so I shall gather you in My anger and in My wrath, and I shall lay you there and melt you. And I shall gather you and blow on you with the fire of My wrath, and you will be melted in the midst of it. As silver is melted in the furnace, so you will be melted in the midst of it; and you will know that I, the Lord, have poured out My wrath on you'" (Ezek. 22:17-22, NASB).

The effect of the great tribulation on Israel will be to burn out her dross as the smelter does to metal. The tribulation will be like a heated furnace melting Israel. It will be the outpouring of God's wrath on their national rebellion against His law.

The prophet Zechariah also makes use of the symbolism of the furnace in his prediction of this tribulation:

> "And it will come about in all
>   the land,"
> Declares the Lord,
> "That two parts in it will be cut
>   off and perish;
> But the third will be left in it.
> "And I will bring the third part
>   through the fire,
> Refine them as silver is
>   refined,
> And test them as gold is
>   tested.
> They will call on My name,
> And I will answer them;
> I will say, 'They are My
>   people,'
> And they will say, 'The Lord is
>   my God'" (Zech. 13:8-9, NASB).

Zechariah indicates that the tribulation will be so severe that two-thirds of the nation will perish in those days.

The Hebrew prophets, then, saw the great tribulation as a prophetic event related to the covenant nation—Israel. They understood it to be a short, intense season of divine judgment immediately preceding the restoration of the nation.

The New Testament broadens the impact of the great tribulation to include all the nations of the world. Christ said:

> "And there will be signs in sun and moon and

stars, and upon the earth dismay among nations, in perplexity at the roaring of the sea and the waves, men fainting from fear and the expectation of the things which are coming upon the world; for the powers of the heavens will be shaken" (Luke 21:25-26, NASB).

John the apostle described the great tribulation as, ". . . that hour which is about to come upon the whole world, to test those who dwell upon the earth" (Rev. 3:10, NASB).

The purpose of the great tribulation is divine judgment on Israel and the Gentile nations because of their sins. This worldwide holocaust will be a time of wrath. It is no ordinary tribulation. The forces of retribution, the fury of demonic activity, and the outpoured anger of God will bring unspeakable distress to the world. God will purge the dross from Israel in preparation for her national conversion and will gather the Gentile nations to Jerusalem for the close of history as we now know it. The details of that awful period are given in Revelation, chapters 5 through 19.

The Martyrs of the Great Tribulation

One other important passage of Scripture relating to the tribulation is found in Revelation 7:9-17.

After these things I looked, and behold, a great multitude, which no one could count, from every nation and all tribes and peoples and tongues, standing before the throne and before the Lamb, clothed in white robes, and palm branches were in their hands; and they cry out with a loud voice, saying, "Salvation to our God who sits on the throne, and to the Lamb." And all the angels were standing around the throne and around the

*elders and the four living creatures; and they fell
on their faces before the throne and worshiped
God, saying, "Amen, blessing and glory and
wisdom and thanksgiving and honor and power
and might, be to our God forever and ever.
Amen." And one of the elders answered, saying
to me, "These who are clothed in the white robes,
who are they, and from where have they come?"
And I said to him, "My lord, you know." And he
said to me, "These are the ones who come out of
the great tribulation, and they have washed their
robes and made them white in the blood of the
Lamb. For this reason, they are before the throne
of God; and they serve Him day and night in His
temple; and He who sits on the throne shall
spread His tabernacle over them. They shall
hunger no more, neither thirst any more; neither
shall the sun beat down on them, nor any heat;
for the Lamb in the center of the throne shall be
their shepherd, and shall guide them to springs of
the water of life; and God shall wipe every tear
from their eyes" (NASB).*

The apostle, having been caught up to heaven, views
the earth scene from that perspective. God gives him one
vision after another depicting the events of the great tribulation. John sees a great multitude of rejoicing saints in
this vision, all of whom are worshiping before the throne of
God. One of the elders explains to John that this innumerable congregation came out of the great tribulation. Many
commentators assume that this multitude represents the
fruit of evangelism across the ages and that tribulation here
means the common tribulations of all saints. But does the
passage say this? No. The elder says that they came out of
the great tribulation. The use of the definite article along

with the adjective, *great*, marks this tribulation as a specific one. It is an eschatological tribulation and not the afflictions of God's people across the ages.

As we have seen in our look at Old and New Testament passages, tribulation and judgment are closely related. The great tribulation is a judgment unparalleled in human history. It will combine the afflictions imposed by the wickedness of ungodly men, the anguish that comes from demonic forces, and the awful wrath of God poured out on this depraved world. The church of Jesus Christ has been saved from wrath and will be raptured from the earth scene before this storm breaks.

Two passages in particular promise the church's deliverance. The message Christ sent the church in Philadelphia implies a coming period of intense testing and a promise that the overcoming church will be delivered from it.

> *"Because you have kept the word of My persever-*
> *ance, I also will keep you from the hour of testing,*
> *that hour which is about to come upon the whole*
> *world, to test those who dwell upon the earth"*
> *(Rev. 3:10, NASB).*

Christ in the Olivet discourse gave a warning that seems related to the hope of escaping the ultimate hour of tribulation that is to come on the earth.

> *"Be on guard, that your hearts may not be*
> *weighted down with dissipation and drunken-*
> *ness and the worries of life, and that day come*
> *on you suddenly like a trap; for it will come upon*
> *all those who dwell on the face of the earth. But*
> *keep on the alert at all times, praying in order*
> *that you may have strength to escape all these*

*things that are about to take place, and to stand
before the Son of Man" (Luke 21:34-36, NASB).*

The suffering church lives in the hope of Christ's coming. The appearing of Christ means escape from the ultimate tribulation and the unleashing of the wrath of God.

The question is raised, and rightly so, If the church is to be raptured from the earth prior to the great tribulation, then who are the believers described as coming out of the great tribulation? The context holds the answer to this question. Before John's vision of the innumerable multitude, he saw a body of Jewish believers numbering 144,000. When the church has been removed from the earth scene, God will raise up a testimony to His name from among the Jews. Though most of the Jewish people will remain in unbelief until the public appearance of Christ the Messiah, some will be saved at the beginning of the tribulation period. Their witness will be universal and the fruit of their evangelistic efforts will be from every tribe and nation (Rev. 7:9-17).

No one can read the Book of Revelation without discovering a number of references to believers even during the darkest hours of the great tribulation. The suffering of those who accept Christ will be great. Many will give their lives for their testimony. The patience and strength of the tribulation saints—both Jews and Gentiles—provide a model for Christian suffering now. The mercy of God is so great that even though God's purpose during the time of the great tribulation is to deal severely with Israel and the nations for their sins, multitudes of people who have never previously had opportunity to believe will hear and receive the message of the gospel.

5

The Restoration of Israel

Among the themes of Bible prophecy, one that is particularly edifying is the restoration of Israel. Jesus Christ is coming back to restore God's ancient people Israel to a place of full blessing.

The prospect of Israel's restoration is found in brief in Romans 11:25-29:

> For I do not want you, brethren, to be uninformed of this mystery, lest you be wise in your own estimation, that a partial hardening has happened to Israel until the fulness of the Gentiles has come in; and thus all Israel will be saved; Just as it is written,
> > "The deliverer will come
> > from Zion,
> > He will remove ungodliness
> > from Jacob."
> > "And this is My covenant
> > with them,
> > When I take away their sins."
>
> From the standpoint of the gospel they are enemies for your sake, but from the standpoint of God's choice they are beloved for the sake of the fathers; for the gifts and the calling of God are irrevocable (NASB).

That this theme is so important and that it therefore concerns those who are Christians is seen by its extensive treatment in the Scriptures. The theme of Israel's restoration is interwoven throughout the entire New Testament. It is taught in the Gospels and in the Book of Acts. It is taught in the Epistles and in the Book of Revelation. Israel's restoration was so important to the apostle Paul that he devoted three chapters of the Book of Romans to this subject; chapters 9, 10, and 11 give a theological view of the restoration of God's ancient people Israel.

Israel's Past

Before we look at what the Scriptures teach about the coming restoration of Israel, we must go back to the beginning to see how God brought this nation into being supernaturally by His power, placed it in the center of the earth as the head of the nations, brought judgment on her for her disobedience, and in modern times has begun to work out His plan for her restoration.

God dealt severely with the world in ancient times by sending a flood. Out of the whole population, He rescued only eight people, the family of Noah. From their seed came all the nations of the world. The earth was eventually repopulated and the very same sins that had brought the judgment of the flood had reoccurred in the new nations that had been born. God looked down on the earth and saw the almost universal idolatry of men. One man by the name of Abraham worshiped the true God. He was surrounded by heathen; everybody in his city and his entire community worshiped the stars, the idols, and the evil spirits. But Abraham worshiped the God who made heaven and earth, the God who could speak to man. Abraham heard the voice of God saying, "Go forth from your country,. . .to the land which I will show you; and I will make you a great nation" (Gen. 12:1-2, NASB). Old and childless, Abraham was the least likely person in the world to take on this task. But without any hesitation he obeyed God, and the Bible records his journey toward the land of Canaan where he was to sojourn all his days. God spoke to Abraham about His purpose for him and his seed. By a miracle his aged wife was quickened and bore him a son. This childless old man was to become the father of nations. And that son that came from his own loins became the father of the nation of Israel. The nation of Israel was brought into being supernaturally by the power of God.

God's purpose was that this nation was to be His community of witness to the world. Israel was to be the head of the nations (Deut. 28). God placed the nations in the world in accordance to the tribes of Israel (Deut. 32). Israel was central in the mind of the Almighty God among the nations of the earth. These people were to bear the oracles of God; their leaders were to be the prophets of God. They had spiritual privileges, the covenant, and the promises of God. Through Israel the Bible was given to us. Through this people God brought Jesus Christ into the world, for a virgin from among them gave birth to the Son of God. God destined the nation of Israel to be His instrument in the world to do many things.

Abraham's family grew to seventy souls and went down into Egypt. Abraham's seed sojourned in Egypt over four hundred years. Toward the close of that period a new Pharaoh reduced the Israelites to slavery. Pharaoh persecuted the people of God, and they began to cry for help. God was getting a man ready for this hour of crisis in Israel's history. Moses was destined to lead Israel out of bondage. God spoke, "Moses, I want you to get over there to Egypt's land because I have heard the cry of my people and I want you to go before Pharaoh and tell Pharaoh to let my people go." Jehovah God, by great miraculous power, did bring them out of Egypt, almost three million strong, and took them into the wilderness and there preserved them for forty long years. God sent food down from heaven every day to feed them. He opened up the flinty rock and sent them water to drink. Neither their shoes nor their clothes wore out. Finally Jehovah brought them into the land of Canaan, the promised land, the stage that He had selected for the acting out of this great drama of history. In that land God established Israel as His kingdom.

The subsequent history of Israel is the story of gradual decline. Though blessed with spiritual privileges, and demonstrations of the power of God, and knowledge of the law of God, the Israelites turned to sin. They listened to the Canaanites and began to hunger for the things of the world which turned their hearts away from God. God had to mete out severe and terrible judgment upon His people. Much of the Old Testament is taken up with the story of God's dealings with rebellious Israel. Jehovah God revived them many times, but they soon turned to sin again.

As a judgment on Israel, God divided the country into two kingdoms. He took the northern kingdom into captivity under Assyria, and then later He took the southern kingdom into captivity under Babylon. For seventy years Jerusalem and the temple lay in ruins. God heard the earnest prayers of Daniel, Ezekiel, and other men of God during the exile. The day came when He brought a remnant of Jews back into the land. They rebuilt the city and the temple but were unable to regain their political independence.

Then, during the days of the Roman Empire, Jesus predicted another destruction of Jerusalem. For this reason Jesus wept over that wicked city. "O Jerusalem, Jerusalem, . . .I wanted to gather your children together, just as a hen gathers her brood. . .and you would not." "You did not recognize the time of your visitation" (Luke 13:34; 19:44, NASB). Israel did not realize that the Son of God was walking up and down her streets. The lowly Nazarene who was none other than God in the flesh Israel hated and rejected and mocked and sent to an old rugged cross. They put the death sentence on Him and stood by while He was crucified.

About forty years later, in A.D. 70, the soon-to-be Roman emperor, Titus, came with his armies and leveled Jerusalem to the ground. He dispersed the Jews among the nations of the world. The prophecy of Jesus in Matthew 24 was literally fulfilled. The ancient prophecy of Deuteronomy 4 also came to pass. Since the diaspora began, Israel's history has been a story of suffering. Awful sorrow and suffering came to the Jewish people in the Spanish Inquisition. In France and England and in many other parts of the world they were persecuted, repressed, and driven into ghettos. During the terrible holocaust in Germany under Hitler's Nazi regime, six million Jews were put to death. They are persecuted today wherever the Communist regime is in power. And yet, despite twenty-five hundred years in dispersion, Israel, unlike any other nation in history, retained its identity.

The explanation of this remarkable feature of Israel's history is God's plan for the nation. That plan is beginning again to take shape. On May 14, 1948, a miracle took place. The nation that had been under foreign domination for twenty-five hundred years became an independent state again. Thirty years ago there was little in the news about the Jewish people. Little was said about the Middle East. But now the Middle East is center stage in world affairs. It is the center of attention in the family of nations as well as the center of divine attention. The United States has spent millions to effect peace in the Middle East, and great international effort has gone into the peace negotiations there. Any peace in that part of the world, however, is only a temporary lull in the storm. Daniel 11 and Ezekiel 38 and 39 show that a whole pattern of wars will yet take place in that land. And most of those wars will take place after the coming of the Lord for His church. The great end-time wars will refine and purify God's ancient people Israel to prepare them for the day of their national conversion.

Israel's Future

The Scriptures have much to say not only about Israel's past in God's plan but also about her future. Paul felt it was important for Christians to understand God's plan for His ancient people Israel. To the Romans he wrote: "I do not want you, brethren, to be uninformed of this mystery [the mystery that has to do with Israel]" (Rom. 11:25, NASB). Israel had not been permanently set aside. "I say then, God has not rejected His people, has He? May it never be!" (Rom. 11:1, NASB). No. God did not reject Israel permanently. Her rejection is temporary and partial.

God's plan for Israel has been a subject for Christian scholars from the apostles through every age of the church to the present. Augustine concluded that God was through with Israel forever. He believed that God replaced Israel with the New Testament church, and Israel would never come back into the plan of God. Augustine therefore saw no need for a literal kingdom. He spiritualized all of the scriptural promises of Israel's restoration. The great Catholic scholar, St. Augustine became very powerful in the church, and his theology was the backbone of Romanism and of much early Protestant theology. Luther, Melanchthon, John Knox, Calvin, Beza, and other early reformers were students of St. Augustine and drew heavily from his book *The City of God.*

Augustine's system of hermeneutics has caused the church a lot of trouble. The Bible must speak for itself. If the Old Testament is to be spiritualized, it is almost worthless to the Christian; but if the Old Testament means what it says in literal language, then its historical statements and its prophetic statements are important for the Christian to know. The Old Testament does mean what it says when it predicts the regathering of Israel into the land where God will deal with her. This event has a special purpose in redemptive history. Jesus Christ is coming to earth again as the deliverer who comes from Zion to purge Israel from her sins and renew her spiritual prosperity. God's plan is already working. The first phase of this movement has already occurred.

The End of the "Times of the Gentiles"

Israel will continue to have great struggles until the return of Christ. This is clear in the prophecy made by the Lord Jesus regarding Jerusalem, her capital city.

> "But when you see Jerusalem surrounded by armies, then recognize that her desolation is at hand. Then let those who are in Judea flee to the mountains, and let those who are in the midst of the city depart, and let not those who are in the country enter the city; because these are days of vengeance, in order that all things which are written may be fulfilled. Woe to those who are with child and to those who nurse babes in those days; for there will be great distress upon the land, and wrath to this people, and they will fall by the edge of the sword, and will be led captive into all the nations; and Jerusalem will be trampled underfoot by the Gentiles until the times of the Gentiles be fulfilled" (Luke 21:20-24, NASB).

In this passage Jesus introduced a key concept for understanding God's dealings with Israel. He spoke of a certain period of history as the "times of the Gentiles."

The Old Testament records the prophecies regarding this period and explains its origin. God had to judge His people by taking them into captivity in Babylon. Among the godly in the Jewish remnant in Babylon was a man by the name of Daniel. Daniel gave himself to intercessory prayer and the study of the Scriptures. As he waited on God, he received a series of revelations showing the pattern of the history from Daniel's time until the coming of the Lord. The first revelation, in Daniel 2, was a great statue that Nebuchadnezzar, king of Babylon, saw in a dream. Daniel was enabled by the Spirit of God to interpret the meaning of the image. Daniel understood by this dream that four major Gentile empires were to come into power. This meant that for the period of history described by the vision Israel would be dominated by Gentile nations.

Christ said that Jerusalem would be trodden underfoot until the times of the Gentiles be fulfilled. In the year 1967 the city of Jerusalem for the first time in twenty-five hundred years came under the independent and sovereign rule of Israel. That should also be a sign to us that we must be very near to the end of the times of the Gentiles. Revelation 11:1-2 says:

> And there was given me a measuring rod like a staff; and someone said, "Rise and measure the temple of God, and the alter, and those who worship in it. And leave out the court which is outside the temple, and do not measure it, for it has been given to the nations; and they will tread under foot the holy city for forty-two months" (or, three and one-half years, the period during which the wrath of God will be poured out on the nations of the earth).

According to this passage the times of the Gentiles will

continue until the end of the period during which Jerusalem is trod underfoot, that is, until the Second Coming of the Lord Jesus Christ. Though Jerusalem is now under Israeli rule, that is not the end of the story. Care should be taken in interpreting events in Israel today. There will be many upsets. As we have noted previously, the final restoration of Israel to head up the nations will occur after the church is raptured and after the tribulation is ended and the Lord Jesus comes on the scene; He then will perfect everything regarding Israel and all the promises will be fulfilled.

The Nature of Israel's Restoration

Christ told us the signs of the time of Israel's restoration—at the fulfillment of the times of the Gentiles, a time to be characterized by the revival of the Roman Empire and the final treading underfoot of the city of Jerusalem. But what do the prophetic Scriptures teach regarding the nature of Israel's restoration?

Israel is to return to the land, but her return will be in a state of unbelief. Ezekiel makes this clear. The prophet had a vision of a great valley filled with many dry bones.

> And He said to me, "Son of man, can these bones live?" And I answered, "O Lord God, Thou knowest." Again He said to me, "Prophesy over these bones, and say to them, 'O dry bones, hear the word of the Lord.'" "Thus says the Lord God to these bones, 'Behold, I will cause breath to enter you that you may come to life'" (Ezek. 37:3-5, NASB).

What does that vision mean? The Lord gave the interpretation to Ezekiel:

> "Therefore prophesy, and say to them, 'Thus
> saith the Lord God, "Behold, I will open your
> graves and cause you to come up out of your
> graves, My people; and I will bring you into the
> land of Israel. Then you will know that I am the
> Lord, when I have opened your graves and
> caused you to come up out of your graves, My
> people. And I will put My Spirit within you, and
> you will come to life, and I will place you on your
> own land. Then you will know that I, the Lord,
> have spoken and done it," declares the Lord'"
> (Ezek. 37:12-14, NASB).

Jehovah will bring the Jews back to their land, for this is the first stage in the fulfillment of the plan of God. God is now gathering His people out of the graves of the nations where they have existed in spiritual and political death. Ezekiel 34 and 36 also speak of this initial gathering of Israel in a spiritual state of unbelief. What is happening in Israel now is only the beginning of prophetic fulfillment regarding the Jews. There are certain things that Israel must have before she will enjoy full restoration. She must have her land, her city, her king, her priest, and her temple. She will have them all. The Deliverer will restore all those things to Israel by His wonderful intervention.

God's greatest concern for Israel is her spiritual renewal. The Jews do not believe that Jesus is the Christ, and their hearts are hard and indifferent to God even though they believe what the Bible says about the restoration of Israel. Recently in the *New York Times* a three-quarter page ad sponsored by the banks of Israel quoted chapter 35 of the Book of Isaiah and applied it to Jehovah's blessing on their land. The Jews frequently turn to the Bible to confirm their right to the land. But they do not see what the Bible says about the Messiah. They have a veil over their eyes and seem not to see or understand. This condition of spiritual blindness will continue until Israel is converted and the veil is taken away.

> But their minds were hardened; for until this very day at the reading of the old covenant the same veil remains unlifted, because it is removed in Christ. But to this day whenever Moses is read, a veil lies over their heart; but whenever a man turns to the Lord, the veil is taken away (2 Cor. 3:14-16, NASB).

In the Israeli public school system every student reads through not only the Old Testament but also the entire New Testament because of its importance as a historical document. Some day that seed of the Word will flourish. When God pours out His Spirit on Israel, the Jews will immediately understand that Jesus Christ is their long-awaited Messiah. He is that Son of David whose right it is to reign. He is the One who is going to give them spiritual life. It is that spiritual renewal of Israel that concerned the apostle Paul in the Romans 11 passage. Israel has already experienced the first phase of her political renewal and now possesses a portion of the land and has Jerusalem under her control. Some day Israel will have the temple as well. But all this is not enough to satisfy the purpose of God. Israel must be spiritually renewed, purified, filled with the Spirit, thoroughly saved, loving and knowing the Lord Jesus Christ.

God's Reason for Restoring Israel

Why is God going to restore Israel? God is going to restore Israel, first of all, because He loves her.

> "For you are a holy people to the Lord your God;
> the Lord your God has chosen you to be a people
> for His own possession out of all the peoples who
> are on the face of the earth. The Lord did not set
> His love on you nor choose you because you were
> more in number than any of the peoples, for you
> were the fewest of all peoples, but because the
> Lord loved you and kept the oath which He swore
> to your forefathers, the Lord brought you out by a
> mighty hand, and redeemed you from the house
> of slavery, from the hand of Pharaoh king of
> Egypt. Know therefore that the Lord your God,
> He is God, the faithful God, who keeps His
> covenant and His lovingkindness to a thou-
> sandth generation with those who love Him and
> keep His commandments" (Deut. 7:6-9, NASB).

A second reason for the restoration of Israel is God's mercy. How great has been God's mercy in giving Israel every opportunity! God left mercy's gate ajar as long as He could for this wayward people. God is going to restore Israel in order to demonstrate to the world His absolute faithfulness to His Word. God made a promise to a simple bedouin shepherd almost four thousand years ago, and now at the end of the ages He is about to make it good. God said to Abraham:

> "And I will make you a great
>   nation,
> And I will bless you,
> And make your name great;
> And so you shall be a blessing;
> And I will bless those who
>   bless you,
> And the one who curses you I

> *will curse.*
> *And in you all the families of*
>   *the earth shall be blessed" (Gen. 12:2-3,*
>   *NASB).*

The antiquity of this promise in no way diminishes the possibility of its fulfillment. "With the Lord one day is as a thousand years, and a thousand years as one day" (2 Pet. 3:8, NASB). And God has not forgotten one single solitary word that He whispered into the ear of that man Abraham. He has not forgotten one jot or tittle in the covenant He made with him. God will move heaven and earth to be faithful to that covenant. If I had no other reason in the world to believe the Bible, I would have to believe it is true because of the remarkable way that God has kept His word to Israel.

Third, God is going to restore Israel that He might sanctify His name before the nations of the earth. God told Ezekiel:

> *"My dwelling place also will be with them; and I will be their God, and they will be My people. And the nations will know that I am the Lord who sanctifies Israel, when My sanctuary is in their midst forever" (Ezek. 37:27-28, NASB).*

God will do a new thing in world history when He regathers the people who rebelled against Him and who were scattered among the nations in judgment. God will not only regather them but restore them spiritually and make them a blessing to the world.

The Days of Refining

Israel today is receiving worldwide attention. Her presence in the family of nations is a mystery that finds its solution only in the supernatural intervention of God. The Jewish people have returned to their homeland in unbelief. Dark days lie ahead for this tiny nation. One more process is necessary for their purification. The great tribulation will bring unparalleled suffering to Israel.

"Son of man, the house of Israel has become dross to Me; all of them are bronze and tin and iron and lead in the furnace; they are the dross of silver. Therefore, thus says the Lord God, 'Because all of you have become dross, therefore, behold, I am going to gather you into the midst of Jerusalem. As they gather silver and bronze and iron and lead and tin into the furnace to blow fire on it in order to melt it, so I shall gather you in My anger and in My wrath, and I shall lay you there and melt you. And I shall gather you and blow on you with the fire of My wrath, and you will be melted in the midst of it. As silver is melted in the furnace, so you will be melted in the midst of it; and you will know that I, the Lord, have poured out My wrath on you'" (Ezek. 22:18-22, NASB).

"And it will come about in all
   the land,"
Declares the Lord,
"That two parts in it will be cut
   off and perish;
But the third will be left in it.
And I will bring the third part
   through the fire,
Refine them as silver is
   refined,
And test them as gold is
   tested.
They will call on My name,

> And I will answer them;
> I will say, 'They are My people,'
> And they will say, 'The Lord is
> my God'" (Zech. 13:8-9, NASB).

The prophets understood that the purpose of Israel's trials in the last days is to refine her and turn the hearts of her people to God.

God will preserve Israel through the awful days of the tribulation period. The covenant nation will be rescued at the end of the great tribulation by the Second Coming of Jesus Christ. In fulfillment of God's promise to King David, Christ will become Israel's Ruler as well as her Savior. The Lord revealed this promise to David through the prophet Nathan:

> "When your days are complete and you lie down with your fathers, I will raise up your descendant after you, who will come forth from you, and I will establish his kingdom. He shall build a house for My name, and I will establish the throne of his kingdom forever" (2 Sam. 7:12-13, NASB).

Christ is coming back to be Israel's eternal king. When Jesus was crucified, a sign was placed over His cross which read, "Jesus of Nazareth the King of the Jews." The Jews asked the Roman officials to take it down. Pilate responded by saying, "What I have written I have written." Pilate did not realize how well he had spoken. It was the plan of God that the humble Nazarene who died on the cross that day would reign as the King of Kings and Lord of Lords! He was and is the King of Israel. He will take His rightful place on the throne in Jerusalem and from that city rule the earth. The nation that has been the tail will be made the head.

6

The Rich Root of the Olive Tree

The spiritual restoration of Israel is a common belief among premillenarians. There is not, however, unanimity as to what that teaching means in terms of the relationship between Israel and the New Testament church in the coming millennial days and in the everlasting kingdom of God.

Early premillennial scholars saw the restoration of Israel as a people and conceived of converted Israel becoming one with the church. With the dawn of the dispensational hermeneutic many became persuaded that Israel would be forever a distinctly separate people from the church of God and that the two would never become one people. The dispensational interpretation carries the distinctness of Israel into the eternal age: the church will be the heavenly people of God and Israel will be the earthly people of God in the new heavens and the new earth.

There are difficulties presented by the dispensational interpretation of the eternal distinction between Israel and the church. How can that position be reconciled with Paul's teaching in Ephesians 2:11-16?

> Therefore remember, that formerly you, the Gentiles in the flesh, who are called "uncircumcision" by the so-called "Circumcision," which is performed in the flesh by human hands—remember that you were at that time separate from Christ, excluded from the commonwealth of Israel, and strangers to the covenants of promise, having no hope and without God in the world. But now in Christ Jesus you who formerly were

far off have been brought near by the blood of Christ. For He Himself is our peace, who made both groups into one, and broke down the barrier of the dividing wall, by abolishing in His flesh the enmity, which is the Law of commandments contained in ordinances, that in Himself He might make the two into one new man, thus establishing peace, and might reconcile them both in one body to God through the cross, by it having put to death the enmity (NASB).

The church is made up of Gentiles who were once separated from Christ, excluded from Israel, and strangers to the covenant but who were brought near through the atonement. The wall that separated Israel and the Gentiles has been removed by the cross of Christ. This passage strongly implies that the ultimate effect of redemption is to make them one. These verses are often used by amillennialists as an argument against the restoration of Israel. They interpret this passage to mean that the church takes the place of Israel as the people of God. But the passage does not say that. It teaches that through the blood of Christ both Jews and Gentiles are made one. That they should someday be one in no way disproves the restoration of Israel in history.

Christ taught the disciples that there would be one fold made up of all His people. Using the analogy of a shepherd and his flock Jesus said:

"I am the good shepherd; and I know My own, and My own know Me, even as the Father knows Me and I know the Father; and I lay down My life for the sheep. And I have other sheep, which are not of this fold; I must bring them also, and they shall hear My voice; and they shall become one flock with one shepherd" (John 10:14-16, NASB).

That Israel and the church shall be one seems to be the teaching of this passage. How then can Israel and the church be distinct and separate in the present age? How can Israel as a distinct entity become the community of witness once again after the church is raptured? The answer to these and similar questions is to be found in a careful exegesis of Romans 9, 10, 11.

Paul, the apostle to the Gentiles, taught the restoration of his own people, the Jews. The theological implications of Israel's restoration was Paul's greatest concern. He left the details of the political recovery to the prophetic Scriptures and wrote the key to the mystery of Israel by spelling out what her restoration means spiritually and how her restoration relates to the church of God.

The heart of Paul's teaching on Israel's conversion in the end time is found in Romans 11:11-18:

> *I say then, they did not stumble so as to fall, did they? May it never be! But by their transgression salvation has come to the Gentiles, to make them jealous. Now if their transgression be riches for the world and their failure be riches for the Gentiles, how much more will their fulfillment be! But I am speaking to you who are Gentiles. Inasmuch then as I am an apostle of Gentiles, I magnify my ministry, if somehow I might move to jealousy my fellow-countrymen and save some of them. For if their rejection be the reconciliation of the world, what will their acceptance be but life from the dead? And if the first piece of dough be holy, the lump is also; and if the root be holy, the branches are too. But if some of the branches were broken off, and you, being a wild olive, were grafted in among them and became partaker with them of the rich root of the olive*

> tree, do not be arrogant toward the branches; but
> if you are arrogant, remember that it is not you
> who supports the root, but the root supports you
> (NASB).

The temporary suspension of Israel has in the sovereign workings of God brought untold riches to the world. The church has been the instrument for gathering out of the nations of the world a people for Christ's name. Paul argues that if Israel's rejection brought blessing, how much greater will be the blessing that flows from Israel's spiritual fulfillment. Paul describes the spiritual impact of Israel's conversion as comparable to the resurrection.

In warning the Gentile church of the sin of arrogance, Paul points out that her spiritual prosperity comes from the same source as Israel's. The rich root of the olive tree is the root for both Israel and the church. The olive tree as a type speaks of Israel's spiritual life. The spirituality of the tree Israel in the Old Testament comes from the same root as the spirituality of the true church in the New Testament age. The root is Christ. He alone is Savior in both the Old Testament and the New Testament. God has but one plan of salvation and that is reconciliation through the substitutionary death of His Son, Jesus Christ. To read into the ages a series of different kinds of salvation is to totally confuse the teaching of the Scripture. Whoever, whenever, and wherever men are saved, their salvation is through Christ. The relationship of Israel and the church cannot be understood until that fact has been established.

Many modern evangelicals seem uncomfortable with a literal restoration of Israel as a distinct people and kingdom because they conceive of such a renewal as a reversion to the system of the Old Testament. God's plan is not to move backward but to move forward. Israel's restoration, says Paul, is their fulfillment. It will be for them the age of realization-in-full of the covenant promises. This they could never enjoy without Christ. Restored Israel will be a born-again people, indwelt by the Lord Jesus Christ and filled with the Holy Spirit. Salvation will be an individual matter. Paul makes that clear by speaking both of national and individual election in the context of this passage.

The plan of God for Israel is not to restore Judaism or even the ancient orders of the Levitical system, but to introduce the glorious gospel order to Israel, His people. The faith and order of revived Israel will differ from the New Testament church only in outward aspects.

The late Bishop Moule, in his masterful commentary on the Book of Romans, wrote this statement regarding the place of revived Israel in the divine plan:

> That is to say, the great event of Israel's return to God in Christ, and His to Israel, will be the signal and the means of a vast rise of spiritual life in the universal church, and of an unexampled ingathering of unregenerate souls from the world.[1]

Scripture confirms this conclusion. Revelation 7 details the worldwide evangelism explosion of the tribulation days when converted Jews will be Christ's witnesses. The millennium will be an age of conversion as well. The harvest of souls gathered in by redeemed Israel will excel all other harvests across the ages. Bishop Moule sees the spiritual vitality of revived Israel as a blessing to the church universal. That could only be true if these two communities of witnesses are made one for eternity.

W. C. Stevens, who taught at Nyack College a generation ago, was one of the courageous premillenarians who faced this issue head-on. Stevens called the one fold "the Church of the ages." He believed in the church age as a distinct epoch in God's plan and in the literal restoration of

Israel both politically and spiritually. He believed in a literal one thousand year reign when Christ would rule over Israel and the world. But Stevens understood the New Testament to teach that redeemed Israel and the church of God would be one glorious church in the everlasting kingdom.

Stevens built his case on the truth that both Israel and the church had one common root.

> How plainly this shows that the gospel age is spiritually a continuation of the Hebrew age,—in fact, its ingraft; that the church is not a new thing spiritually, but that it is the old stock of the true Israel simply reinforced in fruit-bearing by new grafts from the Gentile stock at a time when the natural branches had become fruitless. Let us, then, not overlook the fact that the root of the Church of this age is the spiritual stock of Israel of the former age. Of course, the truth of the matter is that that stock was the Son of God, Himself, who was the life of the faithful Israelite as well before the incarnation as He is of the faithful Christian since the incarnation.[2]

If Israel and the church spring from a common spiritual stock, their ultimate union as one people at the close of prophetic history seems logical. There is no aspect of this concept but what can be reconciled with a premillennial view of our Lord's return. W. C. Stevens believed the answer to be in a proper understanding of Paul's letter to the Ephesians. Stevens says:

> This unity in the universality and the totality of believers is the great theme of Paul's letter to the Ephesians; it is that which he calls "the

mystery," which Jesus Christ "by revelation. . . made known unto" him; "Which in other ages was not made known to the sons of men, as it is now revealed unto his holy apostles and prophets by the Spirit; that the Gentiles should be fellow heirs, and of the same body, and partakers of his promise in Christ by the gospel (Eph. 3:6). It is a mistake to consider that this unity of the Jews and the Gentiles in the same body dates first from this new dispensation; it is not the fact of this unity that is of modern date, it is only the fully unveiled disclosure of the fact. The fact was before held in "mystery"—hid in God (v. 9) but now is given to make all men see what is the fellowship of the mystery.[3]

It is, then, in the Pauline epistles that the truth of the one body is integrated with the prophecies that call for Israel's restoration. Paul maintained the distinctives of Israel and the church as manifest in history but understood that the two are separate manifestations of one spiritual household. He anticipated their unity in the final age. In the letter to the Galatians he said:

> But Jerusalem which is above is free, which is the mother of us all (Gal. 4:26, KJV).

The writer to the Hebrews assigns the same spiritual aspirations to the saints in Israel as those that characterize church-age saints. They have as their common goal the city that has foundations whose builder and maker is God. The Hebrew letter pictures that glorious church composed of all the redeemed.

> But you have come to Mount Zion and to the city

of the living God, the heavenly Jerusalem, and to
myriads of angels, to the general assembly and
church of the first-born who are enrolled in
heaven, and to God, the Judge of all, and to the
spirits of righteous men made perfect, and to
Jesus, the mediator of a new covenant, and to the
sprinkled blood, which speaks better than the
blood of Abel (Heb. 12:22-24, NASB).

John adds the final touches to this picture in Revelation 21. The city of God is described in language that suggests the unity of all God's redeemed people. On the gates of that holy city are engraved the names of the twelve tribes of the sons of Israel and on the foundation stones are engraved the names of the twelve apostles of the Lamb. In that glad and heavenly city Israel and the church of God are one at last and shall be one forever.

Before leaving this subject, the place of the new covenant must be considered. The prophet Jeremiah announced in old-covenant days that it was God's purpose to make a new covenant with His people.

"Behold, days are coming," declares the Lord,
"when I will make a new covenant with the house
of Israel and with the house of Judah, not like the
covenant which I made with their fathers in the
day I took them by the hand to bring them out of
the land of Egypt, My covenant which they
broke, although I was a husband to them," declares the Lord. "But this is the covenant which I
will make with the house of Israel after those
days," declares the Lord, "I will put My law within them, and on their heart I will write it; and I
will be their God, and they shall be My people"
(Jer. 31:31-33, NASB).

Jehovah's new covenant with Israel is readily distinguished from the old in that it brings about an inner transformation rather than conformity to an outer ritual. Christ made that covenant a reality by His finished work. At the last supper Jesus told the disciples that the cup represented the new covenant in His blood. The new covenant became effective at the beginning of the gospel age. The church of God is today experiencing and enjoying the new covenant that Israel will receive in her restoration. The millennial age allows for Jeremiah's prophecy to be completely fulfilled in Israel. The quality of spiritual life in renewed Israel will be the same as the church-age believers enjoy today. Israel will be under the new covenant.

The consideration of this subject is germane to the study of the kingdom of God. The proponents of amillennialism often appeal to the above Scriptures in an effort to remove any necessity for the millennium. They fail to see that neither Israel nor the church can be equated with the kingdom of God. The kingdom is a larger concept and embraces both Israel and the church. That they be united as one in the New Jerusalem at the close of time in no way demands that they be one at every stage of history. The prophetic Scripture rather indicates the necessity of many intervening ages to bring about God's eternal purpose in Christ. At the heart of Paul's argument in Romans 11 is the sovereignty of God in the dispensations. The Lord has set Israel aside and given her lamp to the church for this time. When the fullness of the Gentiles has come in, the Lord will rapture the church from the earth scene and hand the lamp of witness to the revived congregation of Israel. It seems that Israel's coming golden age constitutes part of God's sovereign plan to make public the triumph of His Christ.

Nathanael West, Presbyterian pastor and scholar of the last century, like Stevens concluded that the final stage of the kingdom would find Israel and the church of God united.

. . .What we have is the development, in prophecy, of God's kingdom on earth, by means of Israel the Messianic people. The history of Israel prior to the Prophetic age, it has not been necessary to discuss. It is enough that we began with the blotting out of God's visible kingdom on earth, by means of Israel's subjection to Gentile politics and power. From that time onward, the prophets look to the time of the restoration of the kingdom to Israel at Messiah's coming in the clouds of heaven, and even to the eternal glory beyond. . . . Then comes Israel to the front again, when the times of the Gentiles are ended at the Second Coming of Messiah to reclaim His people, and we enter upon the interval of Gentile subjection to Israel's supremacy, the tables being turned in the age of Millennial Glory. Then after this, Israel and the nations, in the New Jerusalem under a new heaven and a new earth, Jew, Gentile, and the church of God, all one, their distinctives still remaining, their unity eternal, and God all in all.[4]

Christ must reign until all His enemies have been subjugated. The one thousand-year reign will bring about this final conquest. When the last enemy is subjugated and the flock of God made one the Son will present the kingdom to the Father. Redemption will be complete. The kingdom will no longer be measured in terms of time duration. The stadia of the kingdom of God will be over and the everlasting kingdom begun.

1. H. C. G. Moule, *The Epistle to the Romans* (Fort Washington, PA:

Christian Literature Crusade, 1975 Reprint) p. 299.

2.   W. C. Stevens, *Revelation, The Crown Jewel of Biblical Prophecy.* vol. I. *Pre-Revelation Prophecy* (Harrisburg: The Christian Alliance Publishing Company, 1928), p. 489.

3.   Ibid., p. 496.

4.   Nathanael West, *The Thousand Years in Both Testaments* (Fincastle, VA: Scripture Truth Book Company, reprint of 1889 edition) pp. 29, 30.

7

Christ Deals with the Nations

In the Olivet discourse Jesus said that the sign of the fig tree was an indication that the end of history was drawing near. The fig tree represents Israel as a political state. Her revival as a nation is a sign to those who believe in the Bible that the close of that period called the "times of the Gentiles" is imminent. Luke's record of Christ's words preserves an important detail. Christ spoke about the budding not only of the fig tree but of all the trees (Luke 21:29). What do the other trees represent? They represent the Gentile nations of the world. Not only has God resurrected Israel, but He is resurrecting other ancient nations at this time. Egypt, after centuries of political insignificance, has become important as a world power. Greece, Syria, Iran, and Iraq are familiar names in current news reports. The Arab states are among the chief oil suppliers in the world, with the result that they have become a powerful political force. This pattern of emerging nations is a part of God's plan for the last days when He will deal with the nations on earth in judgment.

Jesus Christ is coming not only to catch His church away; He is coming not only to restore Israel politically and eventually spiritually; He is coming back also to deal with the nations of the earth for their disobedience and their sin.

The Origin of the Nations

For the background of this study we must turn to the Old Testament. The Book of Genesis records the origin of the nations. The human race had multiplied and along with the increase in population had come an increase of sinfulness. God dealt with that sinful ancient world with the judgment of the flood. From the survivors, the family of Noah, came the population of post-flood earth. The table of nations in Genesis 10 lists seventy nations that descended from Noah and his sons.

Out of these nations developed a totalitarian form of government. The Bible describes the first dictator:

> Now Cush became the father of Nimrod; he became a mighty one on the earth. He was a mighty hunter before the Lord; therefore it is said, "Like Nimrod a mighty hunter before the Lord." And the beginning of his kingdom was Babel and Erech and Accad and Calneh, in the land of Shinar. From that land he went forth into Assyria, and built Nineveh and Rehoboth-Ir and Calah, and Resen between Nineveh and Calah; that is the great city (Gen. 10:8-12, NASB).

Nimrod established the first extensive political power on earth. He was noted for his strength and his power but not for his goodness. Out of his dictatorship came the kingdom of Babel. He built Nineveh as his capital city.

For the second time in man's history wickedness invaded the nations of the world. Nations like individuals may be guilty of sin. Because nations sin, God must deal with them in judgment. God cannot tolerate their rebellion forever. The plan of Almighty God in making this world was to have a habitation for righteous men. God wants this world to be inhabited with good and godly people. God desires a theocracy on earth; that is, God desires that He alone should rule over the earth. Man has continually rejected the rule of God and become his own ruler. The rebellion government established by Nimrod is the first type of the antichrist in the Bible. In this period in history he is already emerging as a powerful dictator and as the builder of Babylon—the type of the fallen nations of the earth. The governing principles of Babylon have been found in human government ever since the days of Nimrod, and these principles will find their culmination in the Babylonian system described in Revelation 18.

So these seventy nations turned away from God. Under such leaders as Nimrod, their power was strong in the earth and it was turned against God. God's people were made to suffer even then as a result of the wickedness of men who had rejected the theocracy and the government of God.

In the next chapter, Genesis 11, we see that wickedness continued to increase among these nations.

> Now the whole earth used the same language and the same words. And it came about as they journeyed east, that they found a plain in the land of Shinar and settled there. And they said to one another, "Come, let us make bricks and burn them thoroughly." And they used brick for stone, and they used tar for mortar. And they said, "Come, let us build for ourselves a city, and a tower whose top will reach into heaven, and let us make for ourselves a name; lest we be scattered abroad over the face of the whole earth." And the Lord came down to see the city and the tower which the sons of men had built. And the Lord said, "Behold, they are one people, and they all have the same language. And this is what they began to do, and now nothing which they purpose to do will be impossible for them. Come, let Us go down and there confuse their language,

that they may not understand one another's speech." So the Lord scattered them abroad from there over the face of the whole earth; and they stopped building the city. Therefore its name was called Babel, because there the Lord confused the language of the whole earth; and from there the Lord scattered them abroad over the face of the whole earth (Gen. 11:1-9, NASB).

God judged these nations because they rejected the revelation of truth. Up to this point in history all men were enlightened about the gospel. All knew that the true God who had made the heavens and the earth was the God of salvation, and they also knew that blood atonement was the only remedy for sin. The promise of a coming Messiah was a part of the body of truth they had received. Their faith was to be in the coming Lord Jesus Christ. The blood sacrifices looked forward in faith to the perfect sacrifice of the Son of God. They knew that truth. They knew the way of righteousness. But they rejected the light they had. Their leadership said, "We will build a great tower and get to heaven on our own strength." It was at this point that God intervened and confused the languages of men. The immediate effect of the confusion of languages was to scatter the people. These linguistic groups became nations. Over three thousand languages are spoken in the world. The language barrier still continues to hinder communications among the nations of the modern world. This ongoing problem is a direct result of the judgment of Almighty God on wicked men.

The Judgment of the Nations

The Old and New Testaments contain prophecies of the judgment of the nations. A key passage is found in

Psalm 2.

Why are the nations in an
  uproar,
And the peoples devising a vain
  thing?
The kings of the earth take their stand,
And the rulers take counsel together
Against the Lord and against His Anointed:
"Let us tear their fetters apart,
And cast away their cords from us!"

He who sits in the heavens laughs,
The Lord scoffs at them.
Then He will speak to them in His anger
And terrify them in His fury:
"But as for Me, I have installed My King
Upon Zion, My holy mountain."

"I will surely tell of the decree of the Lord:
He said to Me, 'Thou art My Son,
Today I have begotten Thee.
'Ask of Me, and I will surely give the nations
  as Thine inheritance,
And the very ends of the earth as Thy possession.
Thou shalt break them with a rod of iron,
Thou shalt shatter them like earthware.'"

Now therefore, O kings, show discernment;
Take warning, O judges of the earth.
Worship the Lord with reverence,
And rejoice with trembling.
Do homage to the Son, lest He become angry,
  and you perish in the way,
For His wrath may soon be kindled.

How blessed are all who take refuge in Him! (Ps.
2:1-12, NASB).

The Psalmist paints a scene that has an end-time application. The whole world is in an uproar as the nations
gather for a great assembly. The representatives of these
nations seem bent on one thing—the overthrow of the ways
of God. The purpose of this gathering is a deliberate and
willful effort on the part of men to throw off the rule of God.
The infection of human wickedness permeates the nations
with an ever-increasing spirit of rebellion.

The Psalm first presents the earthly viewpoint. The
whole earth is in ferment as men try to throw off the rule of
God. The Psalmist shifts to the heavenly viewpoint of these
circumstances. He pictures God enthroned in heaven and
laughing at the futile efforts of the nations of the world to
escape His sovereign right to rule. God says, "I have set My
king upon My holy hill." That king is the Lord Jesus Christ.
The lowly Nazarene carpenter that the Jews condemned to
death and the Romans dragged out to Golgotha and nailed
to the cross now sits at the Father's right hand as King of
Kings. The Lord Jesus Christ, the King of Eternity, stands
on Mount Zion, and no conglomerate of men or of demons
from hell can ever move Him from His position. For Jesus
Christ is the eternal Victor.

That rage of the nations predicted by the Psalmist has
already begun. The nations of the Communist bloc, com-
prising about one-third of the world's population, is openly
anti-God. Islam makes up another huge bloc of nations,
where devotion is to a false prophet and a false God. Scores
of other nations are animists and spirit-worshipers. The
great countries of the Western world, despite their Judeo-
Christian heritage, are rapidly turning their backs on God,
forgetting that those things that are good in our society—
hospitals, the educational system, the dignity of woman-

hood, equality, and justice—came from God and the church. The culture of Europe and America was built on the firm foundation of biblical principles. But now Western civilization is turning away from God and the culture is falling apart. Britain is reaping the fruits of this course. Germany has already reaped a harvest from it. There can be little doubt that the United States of America is next in line for the judgment of God. Some feel that America is too great, too strong, and too advanced to ever fall. Let us not deceive ourselves. The retribution will be no different with us than with other nations. Only one thing can save us from the judgment of God and that is a heaven-sent revival—revival of purity and power in the church so the living water can flow out into society and bring multiplied thousands to Jesus Christ.

In the Book of Jeremiah, God speaks again of the nations:

> "For behold, I am beginning to work calamity in this city which is called by My name, ₍Jerusalem₎ and shall you be completely free from punishment? You will not be free from punishment; for I am summoning a sword against all the inhabitants of the earth," declares the Lord of hosts. "Therefore you shall prophesy against them all these words, and you shall say to them,
> 'The Lord will roar from on high,
> And utter His voice from His holy habitation;
> He will roar mightily against His fold.
> He will shout like those who tread the grapes,
> Against all the inhabitants of the earth'"
> (Jer. 25:29-30, NASB).

Jeremiah's prophecy sounds like the winepress scene in the Book of Revelation, chapter 14. The shout of God will be like the shout of men that trample grapes. Even today in countries where grapes are still trampled by the workers, the shout of the people as they work can be widely heard.

The prophetic Scripture predicts an unprecedented state of confusion on the international scene in the last days.

> "A clamor has come to the end of the earth,
> Because the Lord has a controversy with the
>   nations.
> He is entering into judgment with all flesh;
> As for the wicked, He has given them to the
>   sword," declares the Lord, (v. 31).

That great clamor among the nations of the earth seems to have begun already. Ferment, constant war, revolution, social unrest, and fanatic nationalism have become the norms. These forces now let loose in the world are creating an uproar that will continue until the Lord returns. God is permitting this because He has a controversy with the nations. He is entering into judgment with all flesh.

> Thus says the Lord of Hosts,
> "Behold, evil is going forth
> From nation to nation,
> And a great storm is being stirred up
> From the remotest parts of the earth.
> "And those slain by the Lord on that day shall be
> from one end of the earth to the other. They shall
> not be lamented, gathered, or buried; they shall
> be like dung on the face of the ground" (vv. 32-
> 33).

This picture takes us from the beginning of the clamor right down to the end of the clamor, which will be the last battle of the war of Armageddon, when the Lord returns. When God gets through with the nations of the earth, the dead will be scattered from one end of the earth to the other. His judgment will be so great.

The prophet said that evil would be going forth from nation to nation, and that is happening in our modern world. Like a stream, wickedness is running from nation to nation. The storm clouds of divine judgment are already gathering. Have you ever watched a storm come on a summer day? The morning is bright and the birds are singing and not a cloud is in the sky. By mid-day clouds begin to form and the wind patterns change. Then the trees begin to rustle, the cattle get restless, and the birds start to move. There seems to be an anticipation of the coming storm. The Bible says there is a great storm coming in the nations of the earth in the end time. Jeremiah depicts this storm as universal. God will deal with all the nations. God has a controversy with the materialism, violence, wickedness, and the principles of Babylon that are loose in the nations of the world; and He is going to deal with them. The storm is already brewing. One form of judgment after another is falling on the nations of the earth.

The New Testament reveals this same prediction. In His Olivet discourse Jesus said that nation shall rise against nation and kingdom against kingdom. Luke's record of Jesus' sermon adds the fact that there will be great distress among nations.

> "And there will be signs in sun and moon and stars, and upon the earth dismay among nations, in perplexity at the roaring of the sea and the waves, men fainting from fear and the expectation of the things which are coming upon the

world; for the powers of the heavens will be shaken" (Luke 21:25-26, NASB).

This dismal picture of international ferment anticipates the coming war of Armageddon.

The uproar among the nations of the world is a show of their rebellion against God. God is angry at the scene on earth; at nations that are squandering their wealth and that are filled with greed, deception, and desire for imperial powers. God is sick of their sins and is sovereignly loosing the forces in the world that will bring the nations to their final war.

The Configuration of the Nations

We cannot fully consider God's dealings with the nations without some reference to the configuration of the nations existent at the close of history as we now know it. In a drama the scenes change from act to act. Before the curtain rises on each new scene, the stage hands quickly move the props into place. In the great drama of prophecy there are some stage hands. God has commissioned the angels to change the scenery. The stage is being set for the final days. Though the church will be caught away before the tribulation, the dark shadows of the tribulation are already reaching out over the earth. The portents of this great catastrophe are already upon us. While the church will not go through the tribulation, it may see great suffering before the rapture.

The first act of this great drama was to bring Israel back into her land. Israel is in the center of the earth. The attention of the world had been in the West for centuries. With the rebirth of the nation Israel, the attention of the world shifted to the Middle East. It is the crossroad of the nations. The oil and mineral wealth of this region is vital to the rest of the world. Oil has made the Middle East strategic to every major nation on earth. God's prophets predicted the day when this tiny country of Israel would be the center of the earth.

Not only Israel and the Middle East but many other nations are mentioned in Bible prophecy. The prophetic Scriptures signify a number of political power blocs in the last days. In Daniel 11, the king of the North and the king of the South are mentioned as world powers threatening the security of Israel. In Ezekiel 38 and 39, Russia and her satellite states appear as a threat to Israel and the Middle East. So the Russian Communist nations form one power bloc. The threat to Israel from the South suggests an African power bloc. The third bloc making up this pattern are the Asian nations. According to the Book of Revelation the Euphrates River will be dried up and the kings of the East will attempt to invade the Middle East with a great army of 200 million soldiers. The critics of the Bible have often laughed at this incredible statement and asked how any country could have an army of 200 million. That question is no longer asked, for mainland China alone has over 900 million people. India can boast almost 800 million. Asia is awakening. Industrialization is changing the culture. The modern world knows from experience that Asia can be a military threat to the Western world. The recently acquired nuclear capabilities of some of these nations increases their significance in world affairs. One of the greatest industrial nations in the world today is Japan. The insignia "Made in Japan" is now a mark of distinction. China is recovering from poverty and moving toward industrialization. The potential of this nation as a force in the world is prodigious. The great powers of the East are getting ready for the end time.

The most important bloc will be the Western power bloc, the ten-nation confederacy in Europe. In the vision of the times of the Gentiles given to Nebuchadnezzar, the ten-nation confederacy has power when the Christ comes to set up His kingdom. In the vision the king saw a huge statue with a head of gold which represented Babylon. The breast was silver and represented Medo-Persia. The loins of the statue were brass and depicted the Greek Empire. The legs were of iron and are understood to represent the Roman Empire. The feet of this statue were of clay and iron and represent an end-time Gentile confederacy located in the same geographical area as the old Roman Empire. The statue had ten toes.

Daniel had a vision of these same Gentile powers in which the fourth nation was depicted as a beast with ten horns. These ten horns represented ten kingdoms from which a confederacy would be formed (Dan. 7:23, 24). The ten-nation confederacy will make a treaty with Israel in the last days.

We will look at these power blocs and the alignment of nations in more detail in the next chapter. What is the next act of this great drama of the end times?

The Lesson from the Nations

The lesson of God's dealing with the nations is a spiritual one. It warns of the malignant spirit of this age! Christians must guard against the spirit of the world. The apostle John said:

> Do not love the world, nor the things in the world. If any one loves the world, the love of the Father is not in him. For all that is in the world, the lust of the flesh and the lust of the eyes and the boast-ful pride of life, is not from the Father, but is from the world. And the world is passing away, and also its lusts; but the one who does the will of

God abides forever (1 John 2:15-17, NASB).

The apostle Paul said:

*I urge you therefore, brethren, by the mercies of
God, to present your bodies a living and holy
sacrifice, acceptable to God, which is your spiritual service of worship. And do not be conformed
to this world, but be transformed by the renew-
ing of your mind, that you may prove what the
will of God is, that which is good and acceptable
and perfect (Rom. 12:1-2, NASB).*

The believer must not be conformed to this world because it
is a fallen system and doomed for judgment. The nations of
the earth are presently under the domination of the evil one.
The powers of darkness have a frightening influence on
world affairs. Christians cannot stop living in the world,
but they can renounce the system that runs the world. The
Christian community is called to be distinctly different
from the world. A problem for Christians in the twentieth
century is that they do not want to be different. The desire
to be accepted should not blind us to the danger of winning
the world's approval.

The last book of the Bible describes in apocalyptic
language the end of God's dealings with the nations of the
earth. John first saw a vision of the crumbling of the world
system.

*After these things I saw another angel coming
down from heaven, having great authority, and
the earth was illumined with his glory. And he
cried out with a mighty voice, saying, "Fallen,
fallen is Babylon the great! And she has become a
dwelling place of demons and a prison of every*

> *unclean spirit, and a prison of every unclean and*
> *hateful bird. For all the nations have drunk of the*
> *wine of the passion of her immorality, and the*
> *kings of the earth have committed acts of im-*
> *morality with her, and the merchants of the earth*
> *have become rich by the wealth of her sensual-*
> *ity." And I heard another voice from heaven,*
> *saying, "Come out of her, my people, that you*
> *may not participate in her sins and that you may*
> *not receive of her plagues; for her sins have piled*
> *up as high as heaven, and God has remembered*
> *her iniquities" (Rev. 18:1-5, NASB).*

Can you imagine millions of people sitting in front of their televisions listening to the announcement that the whole world economic system has crumbled? Everything people had loved and lived for is gone. Pleasure is gone. When Babylon falls, civilization goes down in utter defeat. The message given to the tribulation saints to "come out of her" should be heeded by the Christians of our time, for the same ungodly system is loose in the world now. The prophetic preview of the end of civilization has been given to help believers understand the need for nonconformity to the world. Man's deep-seated rebellion against God is being overtly manifested in his insane and insatiable desire after pleasure, self-indulgence, and material things.

A second spiritual lesson we see is found in Psalm 2, the passage looked at earlier. The message at the end of that psalm is a very strong one, urging that every king and every judge and every ruler and every person on earth worship the Lord with reverence and rejoice with trembling and kiss the Son. In the Orient the kiss was to do homage to someone greater, to recognize his right and authority.

What is the message of prophecy to us? The message of prophecy is that the nations of the earth cannot escape the intervention of Christ in judgment. The world is coming into a period of unequaled confusion. Nothing has ever happened like it in history past. This terrible judgment is coming because of rebellion. And God is saying that our only refuge is to be in Christ, to bow to the Son of God. The only refuge left in the world is in the bleeding wounds of God's Son. Jesus came once as a tender bleeding lamb, reaching out in love to forgive. He came in grace. He is coming the second time in glory as the conquering lion of the tribe of Judah to deal with sin. It is better to meet Him in grace than to meet Him when He comes in flaming fire to take vengence on those who know not God.

8

The Defeat of Antichrist and Satan

No consideration of Christ's Second Coming should overlook the relationship of that event to the final defeat of Satan. Christ is returning to bring His Father's plan to completion. The exposure and defeat of Satan's masterpiece, the antichrist, will be one of the triumphs of Christ at His return.

Who is antichrist? Some Bible teachers take the position that antichrist is a force, but a careful examination of the biblical passages will lead one to conclude that this is a person. In this chapter we will look at the picture of antichrist drawn in the Scriptures. We will also look at the rise of various world leaders. Considerable confusion exists regarding the end-time leaders mentioned in the prophetic Scriptures. More than one prominent leader will come on the world scene in the last days, and the antichrist should not be confused with other leaders that emerge. The antichrist is the most visible leader described by the prophets. The Book of Revelation also describes a trinity of evil in the last days. This will be the ultimate manifestation of wickedness on the world scene. All these will be gathered together at Armageddon. Then at the end of the chapter we shall consider the spiritual admonition that these truths have for us who live today.

Picture of the Antichrist

The prophet Daniel was given a very detailed picture of the coming antichrist.

"Then the king will do as he pleases, and he will exalt and magnify himself above every god, and will speak monstrous things against the God of gods; and he will prosper until the indignation is finished, for that which is decreed will be done. And he will show no regard for the gods of his fathers or for the desire of women, nor will he show regard for any other god; for he will magnify himself above them all. But instead he will honor a god of fortresses, a god whom his fathers did not know; he will honor him with gold, silver, costly stones, and treasures. And he will take action against the strongest of fortresses with the help of a foreign god; he will give great honor to those who acknowledge him, and he will cause them to rule over the many, and will parcel out land for a price. And at the end time the king of the South will collide with him, and the king of the North will storm against him with chariots, with horsemen, and with many ships; and he will enter countries, overflow them, and pass through. He will also enter the Beautiful Land, and many countries will fall; but these will be rescued out of his hand: Edom, Moab and the foremost of the sons of Ammon. Then he will stretch out his hand against other countries, and the land of Egypt will not escape. But he will gain control over the hidden treasures of gold and silver, and over all the precious things of Egypt; and Libyans and Ethiopians will follow at his heels. But rumors from the East and from the North will disturb him, and he will go forth with great wrath to destroy and annihilate many. And he will pitch the tents of his royal pavilion between the seas and the beautiful Holy Mountain;

yet he will come to his end, and no one will help
him" (Dan. 11:36-45, NASB).

The Willful King (the antichrist) as depicted by Daniel
appears to be the ruler of Israel. He renounces the God of
his fathers, the God of Abraham, Isaac, and Jacob, and de-
votes himself to the god of force. The reign of the Willful
King will be characterized by wickedness and injustice.
    The prophet Zechariah spoke of the antichrist as the
Foolish Shepherd.

> And the Lord said to me, "Take again for yourself
> the equipment of a foolish shepherd. For behold, I
> am going to raise up a shepherd in the land who
> will not care for the perishing, seek the scattered,
> heal the broken, or sustain the one standing, but
> will devour the flesh of the fat sheep and tear off
> their hoofs.
>> Woe to the worthless shepherd
>> Who leaves the flock!
>> A sword will be on his arm
>> And on his right eye!
>> His arm will be totally withered
>> And his right eye will be blind" (Zech. 11:15-
>>   17, NASB).

The Foolish Shepherd like the Willful King is described as a
ruler in Israel. In the Old Testament history Israel's kings
were known as shepherds. Zechariah saw the antichrist as
the worthless, or foolish, shepherd. This false leader will,
while posing to be their promised deliverer, sell his people
out. Jesus alluded to this false leader, as recorded in the
Gospel of John. Jesus was talking with the leaders of Israel
when He said,

> "You search the Scriptures, because you think
> that in them you have eternal life; and it is these
> that bear witness of Me; and you are unwilling to
> come to Me, that you may have life. I do not re-
> ceive glory from men; but I know you, that you do
> not have the love of God in yourselves. I have
> come in My Father's name, and you do not receive
> Me; if another shall come in his own name, you
> will receive him" (John 5:39-43, NASB).

In making this subtle announcement of the coming antichrist, Jesus implied that he will be a counterfeit Christ.
Israel, blinded by her sin and willfulness, did not recognize
the Son of God. Though Jesus healed the sick, lifted
burdens, and taught the truth, the Jews were so spiritually
blinded that they did not recognize Him to be the Messiah.
And yet their Scriptures had predicted where He would be
born, when He would be born, from what line He would
come, the village where He would grow up, the miracles He
would perform, and the death He would die on the cross.
The same dullness of spiritual perception will prevail in
Israel at the time of the end. When the false Christ appears,
most of Israel will be deceived by him.

The apostle Paul also gives a sketch of the antichrist.

> Let no one in any way deceive you, for it ₁the
> return of Christ₁ will not come unless the
> apostasy comes first, and the man of lawlessness
> is revealed, the son of destruction ₁KJV:"the man
> of sin. . .the son of perdition"₁, who opposes and
> exalts himself above every so-called god or
> object of worship, so that he takes his seat in the
> temple of God, displaying himself as being God.
> Do you not remember that while I was still with
> you, I was telling you these things? And you

know what restrains him now, so that in his time
he may be revealed. For the mystery of lawless-
ness is already at work; only he who now
restrains will do so until he is taken out of the
way (2 Thess. 2:3-7, NASB).

Paul calls the antichrist "the man of sin." The word for sin in this passage means blatant rebellion, or utter lawlessness. Antichrist will rebel at every known law of God. He will exalt himself as a god and set himself up as an object of worship in the temple. In every way he epitomizes the mystery of iniquity.

This passage in Paul's second letter to the Thessalonians speaks more explicitly than any other passage about the time as well as the identification of the antichrist. The public manifestation of antichrist must await the removal of the restrainer. The restrainer is first referred to as a principle; then in the next verse the restrainer is referred to with a personal pronoun. Some modern scholars, as well as some of the church fathers, are of the opinion that Paul here had in mind the restraint that law and order places on evil.

Another interpretation makes the restrainer the Holy Spirit. From the days of the early church fathers, some have believed that the preaching of the gospel by the power of the Holy Spirit has deterred the spread of lawlessness and the revelation of the antichrist. A similar school of thought sees God as the restrainer and that He restrains lawlessness by divine decree.

A third approach to this difficult text interprets tne impersonal reference to the restrainer to mean the church and the masculine pronoun as applying to the Holy Spirit. The revelation of antichrist would then be postponed until the church is removed at the rapture. The church's power to restrain evil comes from the indwelling of the Holy Spirit. The removal of the church would not mean that the Holy

Spirit was removed from the earth. The Holy Spirit is omnipresent and will therefore always be present on earth. It is the presence of the Spirit-empowered church that will be absent from the earth after the rapture. In the spiritual darkness that follows the removal of the church, the ferment of lawlessness will bring forth that personification of all evil, the antichrist. He will not be known until after the rapture of the church.

The apostle John gives still another advance glimpse of the antichrist.

> Children, it is the last hour; and just as you heard that antichrist is coming, even now many antichrists have arisen; from this we know that it is the last hour. They went out from us, but they were not really of us; for if they had been of us, they would have remained with us; but they went out, in order that it might be shown that they all are not of us. But you have an anointing from the Holy One, and you all know. I have not written to you because you do not know the truth, but because you do know it, and because no lie is of the truth. Who is the liar but the one who denies that Jesus is the Christ? This is the antichrist, the one who denies the Father and the Son (1 John 2:18-22, NASB).

John taught that the antichrist is identified by his denial of the incarnation of God's Son. In his second letter John wrote:

> For many deceivers have gone out into the world, those who do not acknowledge Jesus Christ as coming in the flesh. This is the deceiver and the antichrist (2 John 7, NASB).

The antichrist is depicted as against God and against Christ. He will be a very clever person and therefore a dangerous deceiver. The principle concern of antichrist will be religion. John warns of this tactic of the deceiver.

Across the centuries of the church age expositors have sought to identify certain personages in leadership as the antichrist. Some of the reformers thought the pope to be antichrist. Later many thought Napoleon Bonaparte was antichrist, Mohammed, the founder of Islam, has been called antichrist by Bible teachers. During the Second World War it was popular to label Adolf Hitler as the antichrist. Prior to the war Mussolini was considered the antichrist. When the U.S. Government implemented rationing during World War II many folks thought that Franklin Roosevelt was the antichrist. The list of so-called antichrists is long and includes just about every prominent political figure. John said that many antichrists had already emerged in his own day. God's people should therefore be on the alert.

The Roman Beast and the False Prophet

The apostle John gives us another sketch of the antichrist in the Book of Revelation. The first ten verses of chapter 13 describe an end-time ruler called the beast. The beast comes out of the sea. The sea represents the nations. This totalitarian leader will come from among the Gentile nations. Beginning at verse 11 a second leader is portrayed.

> And I saw another beast coming up out of the earth; and he had two horns like a lamb, and he spoke as a dragon. And he exercises all the authority of the first beast in his presence. And he makes the earth and those who dwell in it to worship the first beast, whose fatal wound was

> healed. And he performs great signs, so that he
> even makes fire come down out of heaven to the
> earth in the presence of men. And he deceives
> those who dwell on the earth because of the signs
> which it was given him to perform in the
> presence of the beast, telling those who dwell on
> the earth to make an image to the beast who had
> the wound of the sword and has come to life. And
> there was given to him to give breath to the image
> of the beast, that the image of the beast might
> even speak and cause as many as do not worship
> the image of the beast to be killed. And he causes
> all, the small and the great, and the rich and the
> poor, the free man and the slaves, to be given a
> mark on their right hand, or on their forehead,
> and he provides that no one should be able to buy
> or to sell, except the one who has the mark, either
> the name of the beast or the number of his name.
> Here is wisdom. Let him who has understanding
> calculate the number of the beast, for the number
> is that of a man; and his number is six hundred
> and sixty-six (Rev. 13:11-18, NASB).

The second beast comes up out of the earth. A better translation would be "out of the land." Israel is the only land God
ever singles out by that term in the Bible. The first beast is
to come out of the nations, but the second beast comes out of
Israel.

This second beast is a satanic effort to counterfeit
Christ. John says of him that he has two horns like a lamb,
but speaks like a dragon. He tries to imitate Christ. Though
he tries to imitate a lamb, his disposition is so utterly
wicked that his words and actions are like those of a
dragon. This beast is then the false prophet. He is a
religious leader, the antichrist. This ruler from among the

Jews will not only take absolute authority over the government, he will be the spiritual ruler of that people as well.

The association of this false prophet with the first beast is important. You will recall from the ninth chapter of Daniel that the Roman prince is to make a treaty that will last for seven years with Israel. It will be this Jewish leader, the false prophet, the antichrist, who will negotiate that agreement with the first beast, the leader of the revived Roman Empire. This confederacy of the Western European nations under the rule of the beast will have gained, for a short time, international power.

The end-time world government will be joined to a world church. The spiritual leadership of Israel under antichrist and the governmental leadership of Western European powers will join forces. Religion and government will be closely aligned in the last days. Association with government and political issues marks much of the present ecumenical movement. It appears to be the forerunner of that coming world church organization. It will be a synthesis of all religions. Even now efforts are underway to bring Christianity, Judaism, and Islam into a close relationship. The church that is determined to remain faithful must avoid entanglement with those alliances which compromise the truth of the gospel. The true church cannot accept the spirit of antichrist either now or later. A world church movement is already building up and will ultimately be led by the false prophet, the Jewish leader in Israel, and the deceived members of Christendom will believe him to be their Messiah.

End-Time Leaders

One of the end-time leaders is, as we have seen, the Roman prince. The Book of Revelation describes him as a beast.

And he stood on the sand of the seashore. And I saw a beast coming up out of the sea, having ten horns and seven heads, and on his horns were ten diadems, and on his heads were blasphemous names. And the beast which I saw was like a leopard, and his feet were like those of a bear, and his mouth like the mouth of a lion. And the dragon gave him his power and his throne and great authority. And I saw one of his heads as if it had been slain, and his fatal wound was healed. And the whole earth was amazed and followed after the beast; and they worshiped the dragon, because he gave his authority to the beast; and they worshiped the beast saying, "Who is like the beast, and who is able to wage war with him?" And there was given to him a mouth speaking arrogant words and blasphemies; and authority to act for forty-two months was given to him. And he opened his mouth in blasphemies against God, to blaspheme His name and His tabernacle, that is, those who dwell in heaven. And it was given to him to make war with the saints and to overcome them; and authority over every tribe and people and tongue and nation was given to him. And all who dwell on the earth will worship him, every one whose name has not been written from the foundation of the world in the book of life of the Lamb who has been slain. If any one has an ear, let him hear. If any one is destined for captivity, to captivity he goes; if any one kills with the sword, with the sword he must be killed. Here is the perseverance and the faith of the saints (Rev. 13:1-10, NASB).

The first beast represents a powerful political figure.

The beast will become the ruler of a ten-nation confederacy composed of nations in the same geographical area that comprised the old Roman Empire. That ancient Gentile empire will be revived during the last days. The beast will begin his rule with the ten-nation confederacy in Europe and will eventually gain universal political control. It is with this powerful ruler that Israel makes the fatal pact that will eventuate in the abomination of desolation predicted by Daniel (Dan. 9:27).

Still another end-time leader comes from the northern region, Gog and Magog. Russia along with her satellite Communist states will rise up against Israel. According to the Word of the Lord to the prophet Ezekiel, this invasion from the north will take place in a time of peace. Israel has no peace now and probably will not have peace until her alliance with the Roman prince. It may well be that Russia will attempt to invade the Holy Land shortly after Israel forms a treaty with the beast. Russia will feel secure that this time of peace is an opportunity to plunder Israel's wealth and gain control over her strategic location. According to Ezekiel 38 and 39, the armies of Gog will be defeated on the mountains of Lebanon. They will never be able to reach Jerusalem. They will never be able to conquer the land of Israel because God will destroy their armies. It will take seven months to collect all the bones and bury the dead after this awful judgment takes place. The invasion of Gog will not be the last threat to that little country of Israel.

Daniel saw also the king of the North and the king of the South invading the Middle East. At the pinnacle of antichrist's power, news comes of potential enemies from the north, the south, and the east.

> "But rumors from the East and from the North
> will disturb him, and he will go forth with great
> wrath to destroy and annihilate many" (Dan.

11:44, NASB).

The ruler of Gog and Magog is not the king of the North. The king of the North is also called the Assyrian. He is described in the Book of Isaiah.

> So it will be that when the Lord has completed all His work on Mount Zion and on Jerusalem, He will say, "I will punish the fruit of the arrogant heart of the king of Assyria and the pomp of his haughtiness." . . .Therefore thus says the Lord God of hosts, "O My people who dwell in Zion, do not fear the Assyrian who strikes you with the rod and lifts up his staff against you, the way Egypt did. For in a very little while My indignation against you will be spent, and My anger will be directed to their destruction" (Isa. 10:12, 24-25, NASB).

The Assyrian would be the ruler of the country of Syria—another of those ancient nations to emerge in modern times to a place of importance in world affairs. The Assyrian will lead a confederacy of states that could well be Arab states. They will make a last effort to take over Palestine.

The king of the South is the ruler of a confederacy of African states. Egypt, Ethiopia, and Libya are all mentioned in the prophetic Scriptures and could be a part of the confederacy. Their interest in Israel may be similar to that of Russia—wealth and strategic location.

At the end of the last three and one-half years of the tribulation the beast will begin to lose his universal control. Military forces will converge on Israel from every direction. The armies from the north and the south will be joined by a new threat from the east. The Book of Revelation says,

> And the sixth angel poured out his bowl upon the
> great river, the Euphrates; and its water was
> dried up, that the way might be prepared for the
> kings from the east (Rev. 16:12, NASB).

The nations of the Far East will also be involved in the final war of history.

These examples point up the possibility of several end-time leaders. The king of the North—the Assyrian, the ruler of Gog and Magog, the king of the South, the kings from the east, the Roman prince, and the false prophet all have a role in the close of history. War will continue in the Middle East until Christ comes. The nations will be gathered there for the war of Armageddon.

Trinity of Evil

Another important factor that helps put this picture together is the trinity of evil. Immediately following the preparation of the kings of the East, John has this vision:

> And I saw coming out of the mouth of the dragon
> and out of the mouth of the beast and out of the
> mouth of the false prophet, three unclean spirits
> like frogs; for they are spirits of demons, per-
> forming signs, which go out to the kings of the
> whole world, to gather them together for the war
> of the great day of God, the Almighty (Rev. 16:13-
> 14, NASB).

The trinity of evil is comprised of the dragon, the beast, and the false prophet. It can be established from Revelation 12 that the dragon means Satan. Satan is the spiritual force indwelling this trinity. His object is to imitate the work of the Holy Spirit. The beast attempts to imitate God, the

Father. The false prophet takes on the appearance of the lamb, in an effort to imitate the Lord Jesus Christ. Satan has no original ideas. He has not come up with anything new since he fell in sin before the world was made. God turned him out of heaven because of his wicked heart. He has not thought up a new sin since Adam and Eve walked out of the garden gate. He has had to imitate. The thing Satan imitates is religion. He blinds the souls of men more by false religions than by intellectualism. The gospel is being blocked today by false religions. This movement has only begun, and it will be more intense as the end draws near.

With every major spiritual crisis in the Old and the New Testaments there was a tremendous increase of demonic activity. Intense activity of demon forces! During Christ's earthly ministry there was an upheaval of demon activity. The early church faced demon forces constantly. A fresh surge of demonic manifestation is occurring in the Western world. In Europe and Great Britain it is prevalent. An Episcopalian leader in Britain said that every diocese in the country was in need of a full-time exorcist. The United States and Canada have been hit with an avalanche of demon activity. An elevation of demon activity is usually accompanied by widespread use of drugs. And we are having that in our culture today. Pastors are encountering cases of demon possession in increasing numbers.

Witchcraft is another sign of demonic activity. On many university campuses witchcraft is taught as a legitimate academic offering. Clusters of witches practice on university campuses. The practice of witchcraft is not limited to lower class people; it is found in high places. Hundreds of thousands of dollars are spent each day by the businessmen in America to get guidance from the spirit world as to their business affairs.

The spirit of antichrist is already loose in the world. The forerunners of the spirits that will come from the mouth of the beast are now at work in our culture. The frog typifies the repulsive, noisy, senseless activity of demons. Out of the mouths of the coming world dictator and the false prophet will come a stream of evil spirits bent on deception. The full force of the power of darkness has not yet come. After the church is raptured, a wave of incredible wickedness will roll over our culture. The intensity of demon power in our time is a sign of the end of the age. God's people must be alert to the fact that false and deceptive spirits are everywhere. Christians, therefore, need the undergirding of sound doctrine. There is need for a fresh emphasis on the power of the blood of Jesus and the Name of Jesus. The end-time Christian ought to be Spirit-filled. The waiting church has at her disposal the whole armor of God to protect her in the warfare with the hosts of darkness.

Armageddon

After John pictured the demons driving the nations by insanity to the war of the great day of God, he wrote: "And they gathered them together to the place which in Hebrew is called Har-Magedon" (Rev. 16:16, NASB). Armageddon is generally identified with the Valley of Megiddo, north of Jerusalem. This huge plain provides ample room for a massive military confrontation. It will be toward this geographical location that the armies of the world will be impelled by demonic influence. Of the Old Testament prophets, Isaiah, Jeremiah, and Zechariah speak of this movement. The goal of the world's military leaders will be Jerusalem. The Lord said to Zechariah:

> "Behold, I am going to make Jerusalem a cup that causes reeling to all the peoples around; and when the siege is against Jerusalem, it will also

be against Judah. And it will come about in that day that I will make Jerusalem a heavy stone for all the peoples; all who lift it will be severely injured and all the nations of the earth will be gathered against it." . . .For I will gather all the nations against Jerusalem to battle, and the city will be captured, the houses plundered, the women ravished, and half of the city exiled, but the rest of the people will not be cut off from the city. Then the Lord will go forth and fight against those nations, as when He fights on a day of battle (Zech. 12:2-3; 14:2-3, NASB).

According to Psalm 2, these gathered armies will go insane with hatred against God and make war with Him. At that moment the skies will open and the Son of God will come out of heaven on a great white charger attended by the armies of heaven. He will destroy the antichrist with the brightness of His coming. The beast and the antichrist will be thrust into the lake of fire. Christ will subjugate the armies of the world by His mighty power.

Stay Awake!

The implication of these events for the believer now is reflected in Revelation 16:15, "Behold, I am coming like a thief. Blessed is the one who stays awake and keeps his garments, lest he walk about naked and men see his shame" (NASB). The hour is late. The threat of danger is overwhelming. Stay awake! When there is serious sickness in the home, the family keeps vigil. Loved ones remain dressed and ready to give any needed service until the crisis is past. The Word of God is saying to us that the crisis of our time is so critical that spiritually we must remain clothed and not go to sleep. "Put on the full armor of God,"

Paul warns in the sixth chapter of Ephesians. Clothed with the helmet of salvation, the breastplate of righteousness, the girdle of truth, the shoes of the preparation of the gospel of peace, the sword of the Spirit, and the shield of faith, the believer can meet the attack of the enemy in these last days.

Thank God there is victory in Jesus. Like the tribulation saints, we can know the victory in Christ. A voice from heaven proclaims:

> *"And they overcame him because of the blood of the Lamb and because of the word of their testimony, and they did not love their life even to death" (Rev. 12:11, NASB).*

With the awful wave of satanic darkness that will culminate in the horrors of Armageddon already let loose in our world, we as God's people ought to be awake, fully clothed, and Spirit-filled.

9

The Unfolding of the Kingdom

There is a sense in which the whole of Bible history is an unfolding of the kingdom of God. Redemptive history is the kingdom of heaven breaking through to touch the earth and bringing about God's eternal purpose in Christ. The kingdom as it relates to this world has had a past history, has a present reality, and shall have a future manifestation before bursting into its final and eternal form.

Premillenarians believe that the kingdom of God must be openly manifest on earth and that the reign of Christ over the nations of the world will continue for one thousand years. The premillennial view is pessimistic regarding the present cosmic order called the world. The premillennial philosophy of history sees wickedness increasing and the quality of life continuing to deteriorate until divine intervention becomes inevitable. The bright side of premillenarianism is its emphasis on the Lord's personal return for His people in advance of the millennium.

Two issues divide modern premillenarians into several camps. The first issue is the sequence of events prior to the millennial kingdom. Some believe the church will go through the entire great tribulation and be raptured just before Christ descends to earth. Another group sees the rapture of the church midway in the tribulation period. The third group expects the rapture before the great tribulation begins. The third viewpoint is the most consistent with the biblical expectancy of an imminent coming. This book takes the pretribulation position and looks for the rapture of the church as first in the order of events associated with Christ's return.

The tribulation period will follow the rapture of the church. This dark period will close with the final war of history and the return of Christ to the earth. Christ's return will usher in the kingdom age when He will literally reign for one thousand years. At the close of that reign, the great white throne judgment will take place, followed by the appearance of the new heavens and the new earth. The eternal age will have begun. The everlasting kingdom of God will bless the universe forever.

The second issue dividing premillenarians is their understanding of the present aspect of the kingdom of God. Some premillenarians understand the kingdom to have been postponed at Israel's rejection of the Messiah. This system of interpretation sees little if any present reality to the kingdom. Other premillenarians believe that the kingdom of God prevails among the people of God today and that Christians are in the kingdom and the kingdom in them. These premillenarians believe the Sermon on the Mount to apply to the Christian in the church age. Both groups distinguish the church from the kingdom in that the kingdom of God is larger than the church in its dominion.

The Past History of the Kingdom

The kingdom of God makes its initial appearance in the Garden of Eden. God placed the first human couple in the paradise He had created and conferred on them a very great kingdom responsibility.

> Then God said, "Let Us make man in Our image, according to Our likeness; and let them rule over the fish of the sea and over the birds of the sky and over the cattle and over all the earth, and over every creeping thing that creeps on the earth" (Gen. 1:26, NASB).

The Hebrew word translated here as "rule over" means "to exercise lordship, to have dominion over, to subjugate." Man was endowed by his Creator with dominion. Adam was a king. He ruled by divine fiat over the animal kingdom and over the earth. This initial glimpse of the kingdom in the primeval earth indicates that God had purposed that His divine government should be carried out on earth by man. The kingship Adam enjoyed in the Garden of Eden was instantly forfeited when he became a sinner. The holy and heavenly kingdom of God could not be entrusted to the hands of the wicked.

Adam's fall left a deep mark on the earth as a physical part of the universe and on human society. The light of the kingdom of God on earth was replaced with the darkness of satanic influence. Since that time Satan has exercised dominion over the earth. That dominion of darkness must be broken and the kingdom of God restored on earth. The whole thrust of God's redemptive plan is in that direction. The kingdom of God must of necessity be a redemptive issue: Christ's coming, death, resurrection, ascension, and Second Coming are all essential to the coming of the kingdom of God on earth.

The second revelation of the kingdom of God on earth came about in the theocracy of Israel. When the covenant people took on identity as a nation and moved out of Egypt, the kingdom of God was once again a reality on earth. When the Israelites reached the other shore of the Red Sea, Moses received by inspiration a song that interpreted the meaning of the exodus. The song ends with an announcement of the kingdom.

> "Thou wilt bring them and plant them in the mountain of Thine inheritance,
> The place, O Lord, which Thou has made for Thy dwelling,

> The sanctuary, O Lord, which Thy hands have
> established.
> The Lord shall reign forever and ever" (Exod.
> 15:17-18, NASB).

God was to be the ruler of this redeemed people. The best years of Israel's history were the years when its government was patterned after God's plan. It was a God-rule, for that is what theocracy means.

When apostasy turned their hearts from the Lord, the people of Israel made a tragic request that a human king be chosen to rule over them. Samuel, who had served the nation as Spirit-guided seer, was grieved at the elders' desire to institute in Israel the principle of government maintained by the ungodly nations that surrounded them. The elders said to Samuel,

> And they said to him, "Behold, you have grown
> old, and your sons do not walk in your ways.
> Now appoint a king for us to judge us like all the
> nations." But the thing was displeasing in the
> sight of Samuel when they said, "Give us a king
> to judge us." And Samuel prayed to the Lord. And
> the Lord said to Samuel, "Listen to the voice of
> the people in regard to all that they say to you, for
> they have not rejected you, but they have
> rejected Me from being king over them. Like all
> the deeds which they have done since the day
> that I brought them up from Egypt even to this
> day—in that they have forsaken Me and served
> other gods—so they are doing to you also. Now
> then, listen to their voice; however, you shall
> solemnly warn them and tell them of the
> procedure of the king who will reign over them"
> (1 Sam. 8:5-9, NASB).

From the day of Saul until the time of Christ, Israel suffered the retribution of her unwise choice. So dull had become the spiritual faculties of this people that when Christ, the very King of Eternity, lived in their midst, they did not recognize Him and utterly rejected His offer of a higher and better revelation of the kingdom of God than men on earth had ever yet experienced.

The deliberate rejection of Christ's offer of the kingdom left Israel in a state of spiritual suspension. The kingdom was given to those who would believe. Israel had compounded her darkness by creating a kingdom hope built on their passion for political autonomy. They did not understand that the spiritual nature of the kingdom of God preceded any social or political manifestations of the kingdom. They were not willing to be converted and thereby translated from the kingdom of darkness into the kingdom of God's dear Son.

There is a sense in which the kingdom came in spite of the Jews' rejection of Christ's offer. Men and women from every tribe and nation have by the miracle of regeneration been ushered into the kingdom and have discovered the unspeakable peace and joy of Christ's reign on the throne of their hearts. This spiritual and internal aspect of the kingdom was no afterthought with God. It was His plan all along. The outward state of things in this world cannot be changed until the inner state of men's souls have come under the dominion of Christ.

The present reality of the kingdom of God is a necessity to the divine plan for world evangelization. The church has temporarily replaced Israel as the public witness to the kingdom of God. The Holy Spirit through the instrumentality of the church is gathering out of the nations of the earth a people for His name. Christ is saving and preparing a people to share with Him the coming revelation of the kingdom of God. The princes of that coming kingdom will be the Gentile saints of the church age and converted Israel.

The Present Aspect of the Kingdom

Premillenarians are often guilty of downplaying the present aspect of the kingdom as though it threatened the doctrine of the millennium. Just the opposite is true. A proper understanding of the present aspect of the kingdom is the only proper basis for anticipating the future aspects of the kingdom of God.

The kingdom of Christ has both a *mystery* form and a *manifestation* form. The present aspect of the kingdom of God is called a mystery because the kingdom is internal and invisible. Jesus introduced His disciples to this truth as He was sitting one day by the shores of Galilee. The Lord had just finished telling the parable of the sower. The disciples then asked Him to explain His purpose in using parables to teach.

> And He answered and said to them, "To you it
> has been granted to know the mysteries of the
> kingdom of heaven, but to them it has not been
> granted" (Matt. 13:11, NASB).

The disciples learned that their preconceived Judaistic perceptions of the Messiah's kingdom were too shortsighted for the true kingdom of heaven. By the parable of the sower Jesus established the power of the message of the kingdom in the lives of those ready to accept it. Then in a series of parables Christ gave a preview of the present aspect of the kingdom of heaven. The kingdom in mystery form is life-changing rather than world-changing.

On occasion in His teaching Jesus dovetailed the present and future aspects of the kingdom.

Now having been questioned by the Pharisees as to when the kingdom of God was coming, He answered them and said, "The kingdom of God is not coming with signs to be observed; nor will they say, 'Look, here it is!' or, 'There it is!' For behold, the kingdom of God is in your midst." And He said to the disciples, "The days shall come when you will long to see one of the days of the Son of Man, and you will not see it. And they will say to you, 'Look there! Look here!' Do not go away, and do not run after them. For just as the lightning, when it flashes out of one part of the sky, shines to the other part of the sky, so will the Son of Man be in His day. But first He must suffer many things and be rejected by this generation. And just as it happened in the days of Noah, so shall it be also in the days of the Son of Man: they were eating, they were drinking, they were marrying, they were being given in marriage, until the day that Noah entered the ark, and the flood came and destroyed them all. It was the same as happened in the days of Lot: they were eating, they were drinking, they were buying, they were selling, they were planting, they were building; but on the day that Lot went out from Sodom it rained fire and brimstone from heaven and destroyed them all. It will be just the same on the day that the Son of Man is revealed. On that day, let not the one who is on the housetop and whose goods are in the house go down to take them away; and likewise let not the one who is in the field turn back. Remember Lot's wife. Whoever seeks to keep his life shall lose it, and whoever loses his life shall preserve it alive. I tell you, on that night there will be two men in one

bed; one will be taken, and the other will be left.
There will be two women grinding at the same
place; one will be taken, and the other will be left.
ₜ*"Two men will be in the field; one will be taken*
*and the other will be left."*₁ *And answering they*
said to Him, "Where, Lord?" And He said to them,
"Where the body is, there also will the vultures
be gathered" (Luke 17:20-37, NASB).

In this passage Jesus warns His hearers of the danger in using the wrong evidence for verifying the arrival of the kingdom. The kingdom that arrived with Christ's first coming operated internally. The empire of man's soul had first to be subjugated before nations were to be subjugated. The preaching of the gospel has as its objective the conversion and subsequent transformation of men and women into the image of Christ. These princes of the kingdom are now in preparation for the day of its public manifestation.

The Holy Spirit promotes the government of Christ in the believer's life. Paul said that the kingdom was not meat and drink but righteousness, peace, and joy in the Holy Spirit (Rom. 14:17). The kingdom of Christ can be discerned only by those whose hearts are enlightened by the Holy Spirit. The believer's personal experience of these qualities of the kingdom is affected by his submission to the King. The amazing thing about Christ's work in the world today is that He is ruling in the midst of His enemies. The nations of the world reject His ways politically and socially. The kingdom of darkness appears to be in control as the lives of men are governed by Satan's system. But in the midst of the reign of sin, Christ is ruling in the lives of His people. The kingdom of heaven fills the yielded soul with righteousness, peace, and joy.

During the internal aspect of Christ's kingdom, the impact of the people of God on the culture and governments of the world suffers many limitations. It is at this point that the mystery stage of the kingdom differs most from the manifestation stage of the kingdom: when Christ returns and the kingdom is openly manifest, all limitations will be removed. The light of the kingdom will penetrate to every part of the world.

The Future Manifestations of the Kingdom

Prior to His ascension Christ was instructing the disciples regarding the coming of the Holy Spirit and their subsequent mission to the world when the disciples raised a question regarding the kingdom: "Lord, is it at this time You are restoring the kingdom to Israel?" (Acts 1:6, NASB). Jesus explained that the answer to that question was hidden in the counsels of God *but* implied that the Father had fixed a time for such an event.

The disciples' question may have been prompted by Jesus' teachings on the kingdom of God during His post-resurrection appearances (Acts 1:3). The disciples had come to expect that at some time in history the kingdom that had been taken from Israel would be given back to the covenant nation. From their limited perspective, the promised coming of the Spirit could possibly be the time of restoration. Jesus corrected their error by explaining the exact nature of the work to be accomplished by the coming Holy Spirit.

While the nature of the kingdom of Christ cannot be fully established by a lexicon definition of *basileia*, the Greek word for kingdom, the Scriptures categorically say that at some time in the future the dominion of Christ will extend over the nations of the earth. Nations are geographic areas as well as political entities.

A manifest, literal, earthly kingdom seems a necessity in light of what we know of God's redemptive purpose for the earth. Israel is to be restored and David's Son is to take the throne. The time, the place, the duration, and the extent of His kingdom are found in the books of the Old and New Testaments. The millennial kingdom is a mediatorial kingdom and must be fulfilled before Christ presents the kingdom to the Father complete in every redemptive aspect. Paul says that Christ is to bring everything in heaven and earth under the government of His kingdom (Eph. 1:10). Christ is to reign until every enemy is put down. The millennial reign is that intermediate aspect of the kingdom that will be presented to the Father at the end of the white throne judgment.

The kingdom of God is a heavenly concept and reflects the repeated declaration that it is God's purpose to rule on earth. The history of the kingdom relates to the earth and its inhabitants. This view of the kingdom has remained unaltered through all the successive stages of its development. The Hebrew prophets by revelation saw the finished product. Isaiah conceived of a great redemptive movement toward the ultimate: the new heavens and the new earth.

The apostle Paul on more than one occasion wrote of the association of Christ's coming and His kingdom. He took special pains to draw this fact to the attention of those commissioned to preach the gospel. In his first letter to Timothy, Paul said,

> *I charge you in the presence of God, who gives life to all things, and of Christ Jesus, who testified the good confession before Pontius Pilate, that you keep the commandment without stain or reproach, until the appearing of our Lord Jesus Christ, which He will bring about at the proper time—He who is the blessed and only Sovereign, the King of kings and Lord of lords; who alone possesses immortality and dwells in unap-*

*proachable light; whom no man has seen or can
see. To Him be honor and eternal dominion!
Amen (1 Tim. 6:13-16, NASB).*

Christ will display total sovereignty at His glorious
appearing. He will have unquestioned dominion over all
who rule; His rule will be both spiritual and political.

Both amillennialists and postmillennialists have their
own interpretations of the reign of Christ over the nations.
These systems of eschatology in one way or another see the
church as infiltrating and purifying the nations of the
world until they are completely Christianized.

But the claims of the above passage cannot be satisfied
by a dominion limited only to the spiritual. Those who
discredit the literal reign of Christ for fear of holding to a
carnal concept of the kingdom are overlooking some basic
issues. Christ must be King of Kings. That designation *has*
no meaning apart from the literal subjugation of earthly
governments to the absolute sovereignty of Christ. This
passage calls for such a time in history.

In addition, these eschatologies leave several
questions unanswered. If nations are of no consequence in
the dominion of Christ, why the Abrahamic covenant to
make his seed a blessing to all nations? Why should the
gospel be preached to all nations for a witness? Why are the
nations to be gathered before Christ at His return? The
nations are certainly to experience a greater impact of the
redemption of Christ than the minimal influence the church
has made on them across the centuries. After two thousand
years the church has not approached any *degree* of
influence on world governments approximating the millennium. Their error is found in spiritualizing the kingdom of
God. The propositional statements of the New Testament
can only be satisfied by a literal reign of Christ and such a
reign cannot take place until the personal return of the Lord

Jesus Christ.

In fact, Bengel suggests that it was the kingdom message of early Christianity which made it so odious to the Romans.[1] Caesar could tolerate no contrary political power. A literal reign of Christ on earth was a threat to the government of Rome.

The amillennial position fails to distinguish between the present aspect and the future manifestation of the kingdom. The *present* state of the kingdom is spiritual and has dominion over the souls of the redeemed. But it is a grievous error to believe that the literal and public *manifestation* of that kingdom will be ushered in by gospel preaching and the moral impact of the church on the culture. The millennial kingdom will be introduced by the personal coming of the King, our Lord Jesus Christ.

The kingdom in its present state does not rule over the nations of the earth. Christ now rules in the midst of His enemies, but the day is coming when He shall rule over His enemies. Satan is the ruling prince of the present cosmic system. While world governments exist under the permissive will of God for the good of humankind, these governments are not a reflection of the kingdom of God. The spiritual forces that influence them are often the malignant spirits from the realms of darkness. No government on earth today is truly Christian.

One final point. There are kingdom promises made to the followers of Christ that cannot be fulfilled until His Second Coming. The apostle Paul instructed the Corinthians that flesh and blood could not inherit the kingdom of God (1 Cor. 15:50). Their inheritance of the kingdom must await the rapture of the church. In resurrection bodies they would take their place in the coming kingdom. There is no way to reconcile Paul's teaching in this passage with the theological position that the church is now enjoying the kingdom age. The early church looked forward to the kingdom. They expected the kingdom to be manifest when Christ returned.

The kingdom of Christ in this age is obvious only to the spiritually enlightened. It is at this point that the coming kingdom differs markedly from the present state of the kingdom. When Christ returns and actually rules the nations of the earth, the glory and righteousness of His kingdom will be as evident to the unbeliever as to the believer. The influences of the kingdom will be everywhere. The social order, the political order, the life style, and even the intellectual pursuits of men in those days will be regulated by the moral and ethical values of the kingdom of God.

---

1. John A. Bengel, *Gnomon of The New Testament*, vol. II (Edinburgh: T. & T. Clark, 1857), p. 732.

10

The Public Manifestation of Christ's Kingdom

Christ will come out of heaven on a great white charger attended by the armies of heaven, as described in Revelation 19. The Lord of Glory with the saints and angels will move toward the earth where Christ will deal with antichrist and terminate the war of Armageddon. Jesus Christ is coming back to publicly manifest His kingdom here on earth. This very important doctrinal teaching has been grossly overlooked in the contemporary evangelical church. The Bible teaches a literal kingdom of Christ and no system of spiritualization should be allowed to cloud this truth. Christ is coming back to earth in power and in glory, at which time He will openly, publicly manifest His reign over all the nations of the earth.

Armageddon will leave the world in shambles. It will be a literal blood bath—an incredible carnage. Cities will be leveled and the countrysides ruined! The political systems will be in a state of havoc! Business will come to a total standstill. The final battle will leave the entire world in devastation. Rene Pache, a French theologian, quotes Madame Brunel as saying that if there is not a millennial reign on earth, Christ is coming back to "walk among the ruins."[1] Christ's return will bring out of this awful scene of ruin a glorious renewal. The establishment of His kingdom will usher in the most blessed age in all of human history.

There are literally millions of people that regularly pray, "Our Father which art in heaven, Hallowed be Thy name. Thy kingdom come. Thy will be done on earth as it is in heaven," without having any conception of what that means. The church for two thousand years has been praying day after day "Thy kingdom come. Thy will be done on earth as it is in heaven." The Lord Jesus taught us to pray this way. This is the prayer of the church, crying for the coming of the kingdom. One of the great tragedies of church history is that this teaching has been darkened by false teaching. Before we examine the kingdom, we will look at the various views about this coming kingdom so that we understand them.

The Bible speaks of Christ's kingdom as enduring forever, and it also speaks of His reign as enduring for one thousand years. The Book of Revelation says:

> And I saw an angel coming down from heaven, having the key of the abyss and a great chain in his hand. And he laid hold of the dragon, the serpent of old, who is the devil and Satan, and bound him for a thousand years, and threw him into the abyss, and shut it and sealed it over him, so that he should not deceive the nations any longer, until the thousand years were completed; after these things he must be released for a short time. And I saw thrones, and they sat upon them, and judgment was given to them. And I saw the souls of those who had been beheaded because of the testimony of Jesus and because of the word of God, and those who had not worshiped the beast or his image, and had not received the mark upon their forehead and upon their hand; and they came to life and reigned with Christ for a thousand years. The rest of the dead did not come to life until the thousand years were completed. This is the first resurrection. Blessed and holy is the one who has a part in the first resurrection; over these the second death has no power, but

they will be priests of God and of Christ and will reign with Him for a thousand years. And when the thousand years are completed, Satan will be released from his prison, and will come out to deceive the nations which are in the four corners of the earth, Gog and Magog, to gather them together for the war; the number of them is like the sand of the seashore. And they came up on the broad plain of the earth and surrounded the camp of the saints and the beloved city, and fire came down from heaven and devoured them. And the devil who deceived them was thrown into the lake of fire and brimstone, where the beast and the false prophet are also; and they will be tormented day and night forever and ever (Rev. 20:1-10, NASB).

This passage marks off a reign of one thousand years in which Christ will reign on earth with His saints. From the Latin word for one thousand comes the expression millennial kingdom. The early church taught the literal thousand-year reign of the Lord Jesus here on earth after His second coming. This was the teaching of the church for at least three hundred years after Pentecost. The thousand-year reign comprises a stage of the kingdom of God prior to its eternal state. The millennium is an age of time and space history and precedes the new heavens and the new earth.

The widespread acceptance of amillennialism dates to the time of Augustine, Bishop of Hippo. His classic work, *The City of God*, articulated a system of eschatology that was to dominate Roman Catholic theology and that of most of the Protestant reformers. Augustine taught that the thousand years was not literal but represented the age between Christ's first coming and His second coming—the church age. In his system the binding of Satan was a spiritual binding. The resurrection in Revelation 20, Augustine took to be a spiritual resurrection, or the new birth. Augustine's interpretation went unchallenged for the most part until the late seventeenth century when premillennialism again surfaced in some segments of the Protestant churches. Then during the early years of the Wesleyan revival, about the middle of the 1800s, postmillennialism was first preached. Daniel Whitby, the father of this movement, believed that the church would bring in the millennial reign by the propagation of the gospel and that after a thousand years of blessing, Christ would return.

The language of the Book of Revelation and the statements of the Old Testament prophets make the return of Christ to usher in and to reign over the millennial kingdom the only tenable position. The millennium is a literal reign of our Lord Jesus Christ on earth. It will be an open, public manifestation of the kingdom of God. Dr. A. B. Simpson, founder of The Christian and Missionary Alliance, said:

> The hope of the Church and the Christian is the coming of our Lord and Saviour Jesus Christ and the kingdom which He is to set up on this blighted and misgoverned world. He has told us that His kingdom is not of this world. It has a spiritual form in the present age consisting of all those who are quickened and united with Himself by the Holy Ghost. But the manifestation of the kingdom is reserved for His glorious appearing as King of kings and Lord of lords. The New Jerusalem is not a product of this earthly clime, but is to descend from God out of heaven.[2]

The dream of a golden age is not peculiar to Christianity. The early Greeks thought they were going to create a perfect culture. It did not survive. The Romans thought they had created a great culture, but Gibbons's book, *The Rise and Fall of the Roman Empire*, chronicles the tragic collapse of that civilization. Great Britain thought it had built the greatest empire of modern times, but we know the sad story of its demise. American leaders are constantly projecting a state of world peace, plenty, health, equality, and justice. Our own great nation has probably raised the highest standard in the history of the world, yet America falls far below the prospects of the coming kingdom of God. No, there is nothing in history thus far to indicate that man can by his own ingenuity bring in the kingdom. It is going to take the King to do that. Jesus Christ will return personally to establish His kingdom on earth.

The Population of the Millennium

The Bible is explicit in the details it gives of the coming kingdom. Both the nature and extent of Christ's rule are explained. There are passages dealing with the population of the millennial earth. With one-fourth of the earth's population swept away in the judgment of the fourth seal (Rev. 6:8) and one-third of the remaining population destroyed during the sixth trumpet judgment (Rev. 9:15, 18), who will be left on earth to go into the millennium?

Converted Jews will make up a part of the initial population of the millennial earth. They will see Christ whom they have pierced and will begin to weep in true repentance.

> "And I will pour out on the house of David and on the inhabitants of Jerusalem, the Spirit of grace and of supplication, so that they will look on Me whom they have pierced; and they will mourn for Him, as one mourns for an only son, and they will weep bitterly over Him, like the bitter weeping

over a first-born" (Zech. 12:10, NASB).

Behold, He is coming with the clouds, and every
eye will see Him, even those who pierced Him;
and all the tribes of the earth will mourn over
Him. Even so. Amen (Rev. 1:7, NASB).

As the Holy Spirit is poured out on them, thousands will be
saved. A nation will be born in a day, the Bible says. These
converted Jews will be a part of that population in the
kingdom.

The population will also be made up of Gentiles.
Matthew 25 describes the judgment of the Gentile nations
after Christ's return.

"But when the Son of Man comes in His glory,
and all the angels with Him, then He will sit on
His glorious throne. And all the nations will be
gathered before Him; and He will separate them
from one another, as the shepherd separates the
sheep from the goats; and He will put the sheep
on His right, and the goats on the left. Then the
King will say to those on His right, 'Come, you
who are blessed of My Father, inherit the kingdom prepared for you from the foundation of the
world'" (Matt. 25:31-34, NASB).

Zechariah says that one-third of the nation of Israel will
survive judgment and turn to Christ.

"Awake, O Sword, against My Shepherd,
And against the man, My Associate,"
Declares the Lord of hosts.
"Strike the Shepherd that the sheep may be
   scattered;

And I will turn My hand against the little ones.
And it will come about in all the land,"
Declares the Lord,
"That two parts in it will be cut off and perish;
But the third will be left in it.
And I will bring the third part through the fire,
Refine them as silver is refined,
And test them as gold is tested.
They will call on My name,
And I will answer them;
I will say, 'They are My people,'
And they will say, 'The Lord is my God'" (Zech.
13:7-9, NASB).

The Gentiles that have been saved through the witness of the tribulation saints and the mass conversion of Israel together will provide the population of the millennial kingdom.

Besides those still living on earth, the population will include those who have already gone to be with the Lord. The whole church will come from heaven with the Lord Jesus Christ at His return. Most Christians are not aware of the possibility of returning to earth. But once the believers have been caught up to meet the Lord in the air they will always be with Him. When Christ returns to reign as rightful Sovereign over this earth, the church saints will return and reign with Him. The believers' inheritance in Christ includes sharing in His mediatorial reign here on earth. Revelation 20 distinguishes three different groups that will reign. John says,

And I saw thrones, and they sat upon them, and
judgment was given to them. And I saw the souls
of those who had been beheaded because of the
testimony of Jesus and because of the word of

> God, and those who had not worshiped the beast
> or his image, and had not received the mark upon
> their forehead and upon their hand; and they
> came to life and reigned with Christ for a thou-
> sand years (Rev. 20:4, NASB).

The first group is the raptured church whose members sit upon thrones and are involved in judgment. They are pictured in Revelation 4, as sitting on thrones in the throne room of the Lord Jesus.

> And around the throne were twenty-four
> thrones; and upon the thrones I saw twenty-four
> elders sitting, clothed in white garments, and
> golden crowns on their heads (Rev. 4:4, NASB).

Paul made reference to the church's future role as judge among men.

> Or do you not know that the saints will judge the
> world? And if the world is judged by you, are you
> not competent to constitute the smallest law
> courts? Do you not know that we shall judge
> angels? How much more, matters of this life? (1
> Cor. 6:2-3, NASB).

True believers are to have an active part in the coming kingdom.

The second group destined to reign with Christ are the martyrs. Those who died for their testimony will be resurrected and return to reign with Jesus.

A third group will be those who refused the mark of the beast and forfeited their life for the testimony of Christ. These are a special group of martyrs from the last half of the great tribulation. So the kingdom includes all this body of saints who will come back and who will be priests of God and of Christ and will reign with Him for a thousand years.

That this reign will take place on earth is shown in Revelation 5.

> And they sang a new song, saying, "Worthy art Thou to take the book, and to break its seals; for Thou wast slain, and didst purchase for God with Thy blood men from every tribe and tongue and people and nation. And Thou hast made them to be a kingdom and priests to our God; and they will reign upon the earth" (Rev. 5:9-10, NASB).

The promise of these verses that Christians will reign with the Lord Jesus Christ here on the earth is an exciting prospect. We are coming back some day—coming back with the Lord Jesus, coming back to this earth again.

The Nature of the Millennium

What will the earth be like when the Lord returns to reign? The Scriptures provide some clear indications of life on earth during Christ's kingdom. There will be changes in the earth, in the animal kingdom, in social conditions, in government, and in spiritual worship and service. The Old Testament abounds in prophecies of this coming age. A particularly striking passage is found in the inspired prophecy of Isaiah.

> Then a shoot will spring from the stem of Jesse,
> And a branch from his roots will bear fruit.
> And the Spirit of the Lord will rest on Him,
> The spirit of wisdom and understanding,
> The spirit of counsel and strength,

The spirit of knowledge and the fear of the Lord.
And He will delight in the fear of the Lord,
And He will not judge by what His eyes see,
Nor make a decision by what His ears hear;
But with righteousness He will judge the poor,
And decide with fairness for the afflicted of the
    earth;
And He will strike the earth with the rod of His
    mouth,
And with the breath of His lips He will slay the
    wicked.
Also righteousness will be the belt about His
    loins,
And faithfulness the belt about His waist.

And the wolf will dwell with the lamb,
And the leopard will lie down with the kid,
And the calf and the young lion and the fatling
    together;
And a little boy will lead them.
Also the cow and the bear will graze;
Their young will lie down together;
And the lion will eat straw like the ox.
And the nursing child will play by the hole of the
    cobra,
And the weaned child will put his hand on the
    viper's den.
They will not hurt or destroy in all My holy
    mountain,
For the earth will be full of the knowledge of the
    Lord
As the waters cover the sea (Isa. 11:1-9, NASB).

This passage suggests changes in the earth and the
animal kingdom during the kingdom of Christ. According

to Genesis 3:17-19, a curse was placed on the world as part of the retribution for man's fall in sin. That curse has never been lifted. In a very moving passage in the eighth chapter of the Book of Romans Paul describes a threefold groan—the groan of God's children waiting for the earnest of their inheritance, the coming of the Lord; the groan of the Holy Spirit longing for the finishing of this age and the return of Jesus; and the groan of the earth waiting for its release from this curse when the Lord comes back to earth.

God cursed this planet for moral and spiritual reasons, and man has not seen the earth like it ought to be since the day Adam and Eve walked out of the garden. But there is a day coming when man will see the earth as God meant it to be, and that day is at the return of Christ to reign. Christ is going to alter the vicious nature of animals. He is going to touch the plant life. He will release the earth from every effect of sin and the curse. The wonder and beauty of the millennial earth defies the imagination.

We also learn in this Isaiah passage that there will be tremendous spiritual effects on human social conditions. The most significant quality of the coming kingdom days will be their spirituality. Some have rejected the idea of the millennium, thinking that it is too sensual and earthy. Can Christians maintain such a position? Did not God make both the earth and man? God is dealing with all of His creation; it is perfectly rational for Him to set up a kingdom on earth to liberate the earth from the curse of sin and to demonstrate in politics, culture, and daily life the quality of righteousness. The high water mark of the kingdom of God is that the righteousness of the Lord covers the earth as the waters cover the sea. The Lord by His Spirit will give wisdom, understanding, counsel, and strength. By His wisdom wickedness will be detected and rooted out.

The idealistic leaders of the Western world really seem to believe that they can effect world peace and justice.

Modern Christians should not be deceived by this humanistic movement. There will be no real peace or justice until Christ brings His kingdom into the world. There are conscientious people who believe that if man can learn enough about human behavior, then ultimately the behavioral problems of modern society can be resolved. That, too, is a lost hope. Increased knowledge about the human personality has not substantially changed human behavior for the good. The increase of crime, wickedness, and perversion breeds misery everywhere. What is true of the science of human behavior is true also of modern medicine. The more modern medicine learns, the greater the increase of disease; so that medicine is now hopelessly behind in its attempt to keep up with the treatment of modern diseases.

The very best modern man has to offer will not change the situation. But there is coming ONE who can! Jesus Christ is coming to earth again to right conditions in society. He will bring about a total social revolution. There will be no poverty, no inequity, no race hatred during the millennium. There will be no unfairness between management and labor during the millennium. There will be proper relationships among people in business and education and every social affair because of the government of the Lord Jesus Christ over the earth. The kind of world that people have dreamed about is on its way, but it will not come until Jesus returns. Man cannot effect it. It will take the working of God's Holy Spirit exhibiting the truth of the gospel of Jesus Christ in the transformed lives of men and women.

In addition to changes in the earth and animal kingdom and in social conditions, the kingdom will also be marked by a new government. The world will be ruled by Christ during this blessed age. The Book of Zechariah says:

> And the Lord will be king over all the earth; in
> that day the Lord will be the only one, and His

name the only one (Zech. 14:9, NASB).

Christ will be King over all the nations of the earth! He will be above all, King of the Jews. When Christ was crucified, over His cross was nailed a placard which said, "Jesus of Nazareth, the king of the Jews." Pilate ordered it written in Latin, Hebrew, Aramaic, and Greek. The Jews were very much offended and pleaded with him to take the sign down. "What I have written I have written," Pilate said, and refused to remove the placard. Pilate spoke better than he knew. Jesus Christ is the King of the Jews, and at His return He will assume that position.

The earthly capital of the international government of our Lord during the thousand-year reign will be the city of Jerusalem in Israel. Emissaries will be sent annually to Jerusalem from every part of the globe to pay homage to the King. To neglect their duty in worship will result in judgment (Zech. 14:17-18). Israel will once again be the head of the nations as predicted by the Old Testament (Deut. 28:1, 13; Isa. 14:1-2). Jeremiah depicts the coming glory of Jerusalem.

> *"At that time they shall call Jerusalem 'The Throne of the Lord,' and all the nations will be gathered to it, for the name of the Lord in Jerusalem; nor shall they walk any more after the stubbornness of their evil heart. In those days the house of Judah will walk with the house of Israel, and they will come together from the land of the north to the land that I gave your fathers as an inheritance" (Jer. 3:17-18, NASB).*

The apostle John was given a vision of the New Jerusalem coming down out of heaven and hovering over the earthly Jerusalem.

And he carried me away in the Spirit to a great and high mountain, and showed me the holy city, Jerusalem, coming down out of heaven from God, having the glory of God. Her brilliance was like a very costly stone, as a stone of crystal-clear jasper. It had a great and high wall, with twelve gates, and at the gates twelve angels; and names were written on them, which are those of the twelve tribes of the sons of Israel. There were three gates on the east and three gates on the north and three gates on the south and three gates on the west. And the wall of the city had twelve foundation stones, and on them were the twelve names of the twelve apostles of the Lamb. And the one who spoke with me had a gold measuring rod to measure the city, and its gates and its wall. And the city is laid out as a square, and its length is as great as the width; and he measured the city with the rod, fifteen hundred miles; its length and width and height are equal. And he measured its wall, seventy-two yards, according to human measurements, which are also angelic measurements. And the material of the wall was jasper; and the city was pure gold, like clear glass. The foundation stones of the city wall were adorned with every kind of precious stone. The first foundation stone was jasper; the second, sapphire; the third, chalcedony; the fourth, emerald; the fifth, sardonyx; the sixth, sardius; the seventh, chrysolite; the eighth, beryl; the ninth, topaz; the tenth, chrysoprase; the eleventh, jacinth; the twelfth, amethyst. And the twelve gates were twelve pearls; each one of the gates was a single pearl. And the street of the city was pure gold, like transparent glass. And I *saw no temple in it, for the Lord God, the Almighty, and the Lamb, are its temple. And the city has no need of the sun or of the moon to shine upon it, for the glory of God has illumined it, and its lamp is the Lamb. And the nations shall walk by its light, and the kings of the earth shall bring their glory into it. And in the daytime (for there shall be no night there) its gates shall never be closed; and they shall bring the glory and the honor of the nations into it; and nothing unclean and no one who practices abomination and lying, shall ever come into it, but only those whose names are written in the Lamb's book of life (Rev. 21:10-27, NASB).*

John adds a needed dimension to the millennial earth scene painted by the biblical writers. The heavenly Jerusalem is essential because the raptured saints have returned with Christ to rule with Him on earth. This divinely constructed space colony fifteen hundred miles square is to be the residence of the church saints during Christ's reign. Modern space scientists are already at work designing man-made space colonies, but their greatest efforts will be infinitesimal in comparison to the New Jerusalem. This heavenly city will provide residence for the saints, and from it they will have ready access to the earth. The New Jerusalem will hover over the earth, and from it Christ will reign for the thousand years. After the millennium, the city appears once again over the new earth. The New Jerusalem will be the home of the saints forever and ever. The dimensions of that city are so great as to provide for all who put their faith in Christ. During millennial days the glory of that city will touch the earth with blessing. All the nations of the world will walk in the light of the city of God for the full thousand years.

Can you imagine the world with every government magistrate a Spirit-filled child of God? Can you imagine a world where every teacher is godly? Can you imagine a world where the devil is bound and cannot inject his insidious lies, deceptions, and temptation? In the millennium the restoration in the earth and animal kingdom, the renewal in human social conditions, and the renovation in government will be accompanied by revival in religious worship and service. The kingdom age will begin with an outpouring of the Holy Spirit. The outpouring at Pentecost was only the first fruit of the Spirit's work. The New Pentecost that will usher in the millennium will far exceed the Pentecost of Acts chapter 2. The millennial age must first be understood in its spiritual dimensions. The Book of Zechariah says:

> Then it will come about that any who are left of
> all the nations that went against Jerusalem will
> go up from year to year to worship the King, the
> Lord of hosts, and to celebrate the Feast of Booths
> or, ₍the Feast of Tabernacles₎. And it will be that
> whichever of the families of the earth does not go
> up to Jerusalem to worship the King, the Lord of
> hosts, there will be no rain on them. And if the
> family of Egypt does not go up or enter, then no
> rain will fall upon them; it will be the plague with
> which the Lord smites the nations who do not go
> up to celebrate the Feast of Booths. This will be
> the punishment of Egypt, and the punishment of
> all the nations who do not go up to celebrate the
> Feast of Booths. In that day there will be
> inscribed on the bells of the horses, "HOLY TO
> THE LORD." And the cooking pots in the Lord's
> house will be like the bowls before the altar. And
> every cooking pot in Jerusalem and in Judah will
> be holy to the Lord of hosts; and all who sacrifice

will come and take of them and boil in them. And there will no longer be a Canaanite in the house of the Lord of hosts in that day (Zech. 14:16-21, NASB).

During that time the whole earth will be bathed in revival. The principal activity in the world in those days will be worship. There will be great rejoicing in the Lord, and all the nations will send delegates down every year to Jerusalem. The house of the Lord will become the house of prayer to all nations as men gather there to adore God.

Worship is fast becoming a lost art in the contemporary church. Modern believers know very little about being lost in the adoration of God. Worship in the power of the Holy Spirit is unfortunately dying in the evangelical church. When the church recovers a true understanding of the coming kingdom, worship will once again be restored. Worship will have a priority in millennial days.

Holiness will be the hallmark of character in millennial days. Holiness will so prevail that the cooking pot in the kitchen will be as holy as the vessels in the sanctuary of the Lord. There will be no dichotomy between secular and sacred life. In the kingdom, believers will not separate their lives into today's neat little compartments, with a secular life conformed to the culture and a spiritual life conformed to God's will. Holiness will be expressed in every part of life.

When our Lord returns in power and great glory and sets up His kingdom, there will be an unprecedented time of evangelism. Many children will be born during the time of the kingdom. People will live longer during those days. The growing population must be evangelized. Isaiah 2 reads:

In the last days,
The mountain of the house of the Lord

Will be established as the chief of the mountains,
And will be raised above the hills;
And all the nations will stream to it.
And many peoples will come and say,
"Come, let us go up to the mountain of the Lord,
To the house of the God of Jacob;
That He may teach us concerning His ways,
And that we may walk in His paths."
For the law will go forth from Zion,
And the word of the Lord from Jerusalem.
And He will judge between the nations,
And will render decisions for many peoples;
And they will hammer their swords into plow-
    shares, and their spears into pruning hooks.
Nation will not lift up sword against nation,
And never again will they learn war (Isa. 2:2-4,
NASB).

The pattern of evangelism described by Isaiah differs from the pattern of this dispensation. In the church age the order is to go into all the world and preach the gospel. The order in the millennium will be the reverse of that. The people of the world will be so amazed at the grace of God, that they will come seeking the righteousness of God. Men will be so moved by what they see of the wonder and glory of God that multitudes will be saved.

The one thousand-year reign of Christ will compel the cultures and governments of the world to conform to God's standards of righteousness. The kingdom age will terminate with the temporary release of Satan. This will test the profession of men on earth. One cannot in any age be a true child of God without the work of regeneration and the cleansing of the blood of Christ. During the millennium people will be saved by the grace of God, just as they are now. Some people will appear to be saved but will not experience a heart change. They will live right because of the pressures placed on them by influences of the kingdom. But as soon as that pressure is gone, their true spiritual condition will become obvious. They will readily turn to Satan when he appears.

The millennium, then, is marked by the reign of Christ and the renewal, restoration, and revival of all aspects of the present fallen world and humanity. It is a time especially marked by spirituality—a time of evangelism and a time of open manifestation of the righteousness of God in human society.

Until He Comes

The reign of Christ will be shared by His followers. Revelation 1:6 says that Christ loved us, washed us from our sins, and made us kings and priests unto God. Every Christian is destined to be a king-priest in the everlasting kingdom of God. The believer should not lose sight of the fact that the thousand years is not all there is to the kingdom. The thousand-year reign is only one stage of the everlasting kingdom. The kingdom goes on through the endless ages of eternity to come, and every true child of God is a prince in that kingdom. Christians are destined to be kings. Adam was given dominion and lost it because of sin. Man's crown has been restored by the redemption of Christ. The purpose of God is to make all His sons crown princes able to rule with Christ in that day.

That fact has a bearing on what is happening in the lives of Christians right now. It is this divine purpose that makes it so important for the child of God to be active in ministry and service to others for Christ's sake. God is shaping our lives with a view to the future. What is happening to a Christian today has a bearing on what his role may be in the coming kingdom. Our troubles would be easier to bear, our lives would be different and much richer if we understood that truth. A crown prince cannot live like other people. When the crown prince of Great Britain is born, he is a marked child from the day of his birth. He is different from other children. His education, his way of dress, what he is taught in the home, his sports life, his activities, his leisure time—everything about his life is planned to prepare him to be king. God makes the believer a crown prince and he cannot be like other people any longer. God has a special plan for him. To rebel at any phase of God's will is to suffer the loss of some degree of princely service in the coming kingdom.

Jesus gave a parable that explains this truth. He wanted His followers to understand that although the full manifestation of the kingdom of God would not come until the future, the servants were responsible to carry out the tasks the Lord had given them until He returned.

> He said therefore, "A certain nobleman went to a distant country to receive a kingdom for himself, and then return. And he called ten of his slaves, and gave them ten minas ₍or, ten pounds₎, and said to them, 'Do business with this until I come back.' But his citizens hated him, and sent a delegation after him, saying, 'We do not want this man to reign over us.' And it came about that when he returned, after receiving the kingdom, he ordered that these slaves, to whom he had given the money, be called to him in order that he might know what business they had done. And the first appeared, saying, 'Master, your mina has made ten minas more.' And he said to him, 'Well done, good slave, because you have been faithful in a very little thing, be in authority over ten cities.' And the second came, saying, 'Your

mina, master, has made five minas.' And he said to him also, 'And you are to be over five cities.' And another came, saying, 'Master, behold your mina, which I kept put away in a handkerchief; for I was afraid of you, because you are an exacting man; you take up what you did not lay down, and reap what you did not sow.' He said to him, 'By your own words I will judge you, you worthless slave. Did you know that I am an exacting man, taking up what I did not lay down, and reaping what I did not sow? Then why did you not put the money in the bank, and having come, I would have collected it with interest?' And he said to the bystanders, 'Take the mina away from him, and give it to the one who has the ten minas.' And they said to him, 'Master, he has ten minas already.' I tell you, that to everyone who has shall more be given, but from the one who does not have, even what he does have shall be taken away. But these enemies of mine, who did not want me to reign over them, bring them here, and slay them in my presence" (Luke 19:12-27, NASB).

This parable makes the point that the kingdom is delayed until the king's return. He left his household in charge of servants and gave each of them some money. Upon his return the servants were required to give an accounting of the master's money entrusted to their care. The money represents the investment of the grace of God in believers. There is something of the divine life, power, blessing, and the grace of Jesus in every Christian. That divine deposit has the capability to multiply and to grow and produce something for the glory of God. When the King comes back, He is going to determine where we fit into the kingdom plan by evaluating what we have done with that deposit of grace we received. Some will rule over ten cities; others over five; others will not rule because they have lost their right to rule. The present circumstance is the proving ground for one's ministry in the future kingdom. No Christian who elects to be merely a spectator can expect to have a place of ministry in the coming kingdom of God. God's ruling princes are all servants. It may well be that the most humble ministries in this age will develop the capacities needed for the greatest ministries in the kingdom.

The spiritual issues suggested by the doctrine of the millennium remove any notion that the thousand-year reign is carnal and therefore unworthy. The public manifestation of the kingdom of God will be the outworking in human society of the inner grace of total submission to the Lord Jesus Christ.

1. Rene Pache, *The Return of Jesus Christ* (Chicago: Moody Press, 1955), p. 381.
2. Albert B. Simpson, *The Old Faith and the New Gospels* (Harrisburg: Christian Publications, Inc., reprint 1966), p. 68.

11

The Judgment of the Wicked

Christ is Lord of all; He is the ultimate authority in the universe. All the nations must submit to His authority and rule, and He deals with men and nations by judgment. When He has dealt with the nations and destroyed the antichrist, He will bind Satan and begin His kingdom here on earth. For one thousand years there will be peace, righteousness, and the manifest glory of the Lord Jesus Christ on the earth's scene. His blood-washed church will share His reign during that glorious period. When the millennium draws to a close, Christ will set up His judgment throne.

Among modern people the idea of judgment has become repugnant. But the doctrine of judgment is to be found in the Bible and is an integral part of the teaching of Christ's return. And the principle of judgment can be found in human affairs and in world history. Judgment is a truth with which men must reckon.

The Principle of Judgment

The reasonableness of judgment can be observed in human affairs. The actions of men often carry their own inherent retribution. The individual who destroys his body with alcohol usually pays the price for it while he is still alive. The person who is careless with and indifferent about his money suffers poverty. People who ignore the laws of bodily health ultimately suffer the retribution of illness in their bodies. Those people who neglect the proper rules of mental health have their retribution in mental illness. Nations, like individuals, also experience retribution for their wrong actions. The principle of retribution is to be found in the social, political, and natural world. It is self-evident in human experience and argues for the same reality in the spiritual realm.

World history offers another proof of the principle of judgment. One authority said that the history of the world is one continuous judgment. Biblical history gives ample illustrations of this truth. The first generations of men became so terribly wicked that God had to destroy them with a universal flood. In that catastrophe the human race was destroyed with the exception of the eight people rescued by the ark. Sodom and Gomorrah, those wicked cities of the plain, so totally rebelled against the moral order of God that heaven could stand it no longer. Fire and brimstone fell from heaven upon those cities, obliterating them from the face of the earth. Recently archaeologists have discovered in the Middle East an ancient empire whose literature names Sodom and Gomorrah. They were real cities; their judgment was not a myth. Just as that judgment really happened, so will the coming judgment take place.

Secular history tells a similar story of repeated judgments. The twentieth century is no exception. Germany is reaping retribution for the awful atrocities committed against the Jews by Hitler's regime. The great British Empire, once the fortress of righteousness and the defender of the faith, has turned away from God, and the subsequent retribution of her spiritual decline has been a political decline. Since 1900 the world has been plagued with one judgment on top of another: World War I, World War II, the Korean War, and the Viet Nam War. War never ceases. Africa and the Middle East seem never to be free of armed conflict. The Western Hemisphere has almost constant military conflict. The judgment of God is falling on the nations. These judgments are only a foretaste of that ultimate judgment when Jesus Christ comes back to earth.

The Theme of Judgment in the Revelation

Following a series of judgments from the very beginning of his vision recorded in the Book of Revelation, John pictures this final judgment scene.

> And when the thousand years are completed, Satan will be released from his prison, and will come out to deceive the nations which are in the four corners of the earth, Gog and Magog, to gather them together for the war; the number of them is like the sand of the seashore. And they came up on the broad plain of the earth and surrounded the camp of the saints and the beloved city, and fire came down from heaven and devoured them. And the devil who deceived them was thrown into the lake of fire and brimstone, where the beast and the false prophet are also; and they will be tormented day and night forever and ever. And I saw a great white throne and Him who sat upon it, from whose presence earth and heaven fled away, and no place was found for them. And I saw the dead, the great and the small, standing before the throne, and the books were opened; and another book was opened, which is the book of life; and the dead were judged from the things which were written in the books, according to their deeds. And the sea gave up the dead which were in it, and death and Hades gave up the dead which were in them; and they were judged, every one of them according to their deeds. And death and Hades were thrown into the lake of fire. This is the second

death, the lake of fire. And if anyone's name was
not found written in the book of life, he was
thrown into the lake of fire (Rev. 20:7-15, NASB).

This scene of final judgment is the most awesome vision that has ever come before a human mind.

John had experienced series of revelations that prepared him for this vision. At the beginning of the Book of Revelation, John was in the Spirit on the Lord's Day when he heard a voice speaking behind him. John turned to see who was speaking and before his eyes stood the risen Christ in all His splendor and glory. The description of Christ found in that vision depicts Him as a judge. His feet are like brass, the metal that symbolizes judgment. The Judge is standing in the midst of the churches. Peter said that judgment begins at the house of God (1 Pet. 4:17). As the praying, repentant church hears the message of Christ, the Judge, and judges itself, revival comes. If God's people will listen to the Judge who is walking among the churches, they will experience renewal and blessing. In anticipation of His soon return, the Lord Jesus walks with loving concern among His churches.

John was soon caught away from the earth's scene into the throne room of heaven and there saw God upon His throne. In the hand of the Almighty was a book, sealed within and without. An announcement was made. "Who is worthy to open the book and to break its seals?" A silence fell over heaven. There was no one in heaven and no one in earth and no one under the earth that could answer the challenge. John was so moved by the situation that he began to weep. One of the twenty-four elders came to him and said, "John, don't weep. Look, the Lamb is coming!" John lifted up his eyes and saw the Lord Jesus. The Lord Jesus walked up to the Father's throne and took the sealed book in His hands. That book was the title deed of the earth.

It was and is the right of Jesus Christ, the Son of God, to possess the earth. The earth He had made had long been under the power of sin and Satan. It was because of this earth's bondage that the Son of God came out of heaven and took on a human body and died for the sins of the world. Having destroyed the power of sin at the cross, Jesus rose from the grave and went back to heaven. As the triumphant Redeemer, Christ took up the title deed of the earth. Christ took the scroll and began to break the seals. There were seven seals in all. Out of the seven seals came seven trumpets and out of the seven trumpets came seven vials of the wrath of God. The seals, the trumpets, and the vials make up a sequence of judgments.

At this point in prophetic history the Son of God declares His purpose to take over the earth again. The church, already raptured from the earth's scene, stands by her risen Lord in heaven as the judgments are poured out on Israel and the nations. The anguish and suffering of the subsequent years of tribulation are so intense that for the sake of the elect they are cut short. What dark and terrifying days those are for the nations of the world. After the last vial of wrath is poured out, there is one more judgment before the millennium begins—Armageddon. The evil spirits have driven the nations toward Armageddon. The Lord Jesus Christ comes with the armies of heaven and destroys the military power of the earth at that final battle. Christ then sets up His kingdom and with His saints rules the world for one thousand years (Rev. 20:4).

By these many visions of judgment John has been prepared for the vision of the final judgment. When the thousand years are ended, Satan will be released again for a brief period. This event will test the reality of the profession of those who turned to the gospel during the millennium. Those who only pretend to be righteous will immediately follow Satan. The forces of evil will prepare to attack the city of God. Fire will fall out of heaven and, by this extraordinary judgment, destroy that army instantaneously. This judgment will be comparable to that meted out to Sodom and Gomorrah. Jude says that the fire which destroyed Sodom and Gomorrah was hell fire. In the world's last hour, when the armies of Gog and Magog, driven by Satan, come against the city of God, hell will once again belch out her fire and destroy Gog and Magog in an awful judgment (Rev. 20:7-10).

The Great White Throne Judgment

The next prophetic scene is that of the great white throne. God Almighty is about to judge men. Notice that it is a *great white throne.* The Bible puts this profound truth in very simple language. It is *great* because it is the throne of the Almighty. It is *white* because white is the best representation of righteousness. God's right to judge rests on more than His authority and power to judge. He is morally pure and can judge in absolute righteousness. The great white throne will be a judgment by the true, holy, and loving God.

Some people have difficulty comprehending divine love and judgment as related actions. God is not a lopsided personality; He has a perfect balance in His personality. He is a God of love, but at the same time He is a God of justice. As the God of justice, He cannot overlook sin. God will act in judgment as surely as He has acted in love. As surely as His Son came as a gentle Lamb to save sinners, so His Son is coming as the roaring Lion of the Tribe of Judah to mete out the judgment of God on sinners. The Bible says He is coming as a flaming fire to take vengeance on those who do not know God and do not believe the gospel (2 Thess. 1:7-8). God will deal with men in severe judgment and He will complete the work at the great white throne.

John's account of the judgment scene opens with the statement, "I saw a great white throne and Him who sat upon it, from whose presence earth and heaven fled away" (Rev. 20:11, NASB). When the throne was set for judgment the heaven and the earth fled away! This description would be unintelligible if the Scriptures did not speak of it elsewhere. The apostle Peter was given by inspiration an accounting of just how the earth and the heavens fled away. Peter says:

> But the day of the Lord will come like a thief, in which the heavens will pass away with a roar and the elements will be destroyed with intense heat, and the earth and its works will be burned up (2 Pet. 3:10, NASB).

The earth and its atmosphere will undergo this baptism of fire! The writer of Hebrews says,

> And His voice shook the earth then, but now He has promised, saying, "Yet once more I will shake not only the earth, but also the heaven." And this expression, "Yet once more," denotes the removing of those things which can be shaken, as of created things, in order that those things which cannot be shaken may remain. Therefore, since we receive a kingdom which cannot be shaken, let us show gratitude, by which we may offer to God an acceptable service with reverence and awe; for our God is a consuming fire (Heb. 12:26-29, NASB).

When the judgment throne has been set and Christ is ready to begin the judgment, the heavens and the earth as we know them will literally disappear in a great atomic explosion. The language of 2 Peter 3 in the original uses the word for elements which basically means "atom." The passage implies, then, that there will be an atomic explosion. God knew about splitting atoms long before modern science discovered it. He was able to give Peter an accurate description of such an explosion two millenniums before the atomic age. God will purge the present earth and heavens and reconstitute them into the new heavens and the new earth.

John's account next pictures the books of deeds and the book of life. God is keeping an accurate record of the actions of men. These records are referred to as the books. Many books make up this sordid account of human failure. God Almighty will be upon His throne when the books are opened. All sinners will be summoned to stand before Him. These books will be opened while the angels and all the saints of all the ages stand there. Every intelligent being in the universe will listen to the somber recitation of actual sins.

There will be no saints judged at this white throne. The saints will be sitting with the Son of God in the judgment. That is a great thought to contemplate. This is the judgment of the unconverted. This is a judgment of those who have been bound in hell and agony, reserved, according to 2 Peter 2, under punishment for judgment. There are souls who have already been gnawing their tongues in agony in hell for five or six thousand years waiting for the judgment.

What anguish and embarrassment in that awful hour when, standing naked before the eyes of the universe, the sinner hears God read off his record and hears his condemnation into hell! He will behold the destruction of everything he has trusted in all his life. The man who has lived to feed his stomach, satisfy his passions, and lay up money in the bank will in that hour watch it all go up in smoke. A part of the agony of hell will be his memory of that experience.

The unrepentant sinner will never know the joy of the world to come; he will have only the recollection of the destruction of this present evil world.

God will not judge on feelings. God does not judge on the basis of "I don't like that fellow," or, "I'm not very happy with that fellow." God's judgment will be fair in that it will be based on written records of man's behavior. There are no errors in God's records, only truth. There will be no defense attorneys at that judgment bar. There will be no appeals to a higher court. The court of heaven will act in absolute justice, and the evidence will be so overwhelmingly clear that no one, saint or sinner, will question the justice of God in what He is doing. There will not be one sinner in hell who does not know that he ought to be there. There will not be one sinner in hell who does not realize that God was right, that the gospel was true, that Jesus died for him, that God did love him and wanted to help him. And the condemned sinner will have all eternity to think about the foolish choice of rejecting Almighty God in favor of the things of time and sense and pleasure. How foolish to have passed up all the glories of eternity in favor of the pleasures of sin for a season!

The books of deeds will not be the only books opened in the judgment day. God will also open the book of life. Each one judged will be checked against the book of life. If his name is in the book of life he cannot come under judgment! No doubt this scene was in the hymn writer's thoughts when he wrote,

> Is my name written there,
> On the page white and fair?
> In the book of Thy kingdom,
> Is my name written there?

Jesus once said to those who came rejoicing that they could

cast out demons, "Do not rejoice in this, that the spirits are subject to you, but rejoice that your names are recorded in heaven" (Luke 10:20, NASB). The certainty of being enrolled in the book of life is man's greatest joy. Biblical salvation is so sure, so blessed, and so full that we can know better than we know anything else that our names are written down in the Lamb's Book of Life.

John's account in Revelation 20, also reveals that in that day death and hell shall give up the dead that are in them. The sea shall also yield its dead. It will not matter how long people have been dead or where their bodies have been scattered over the earth. Every person will be resurrected and stand before God. After Hades, the abode of the dead, has been emptied and the judgment of each sinner has been completed, the condemned will pass into the lake of fire. The Scripture calls this the second death. Once in the lake of fire there can be no change. The burning shall be forever and ever. The Bible teaches eternal punishment as clearly as it teaches eternal life. The same Greek word that gives the believer eternal hope assures the Christ-rejector of eternal damnation. The realization of such an awful possibility should drive the thoughtful soul to the foot of the cross.

John gives a sevenfold picture of those who will go to a devil's hell:

> "But for the cowardly and unbelieving and abominable and murderers and immoral persons and sorcerers and idolaters and all liars, their part will be in the lake that burns with fire and brimstone, which is the second death" (Rev. 21:8, NASB).

Then John gives one final glimpse of the doomed in the last chapter of the Book of Revelation.

> *Outside are the dogs and the sorcerers and the immoral persons and the murderers and the idolators, and everyone who loves and practices lying (Rev. 22:15, NASB).*

That is the most devastating Scripture in the whole Bible. How haunting and melancholy is that word *outside*. Have you ever been locked out? The Bible says there will be a great host that are going to be locked outside the city of God—locked out for eternity. Their cries will never be heard again in the city of God. They will be separated forever. Oh, the loneliness of hell! It is outside the door of the everlasting kingdom.

John moves from that awful scene of the judgment of God to the city of God.

> *And I saw a new heaven and a new earth; for the first heaven and the first earth passed away, and there is no longer any sea. And I saw the holy city, new Jerusalem, coming down out of heaven from God, made ready as a bride adorned for her husband. And I heard a loud voice from the throne, saying, "Behold, the tabernacle of God is among men, and He shall dwell among them, and they shall be His people, and God Himself shall be among them, and He shall wipe away every tear from their eyes; and there shall no longer be any death; there shall no longer be any mourning, or crying, or pain; the first things have passed away" (Rev. 21:1-4, NASB).*

Can you imagine a world where there is no night? Can you imagine a world where there is no sickness? Where there is no fear? Where there is never a tear? And never a sorrow? Never a heartache? Never a tinge of conscience? Never a feeling of guilt? Such a better country is the prospect of biblical salvation.

God has already done everything a holy God could do to reconcile sinners to Himself. And He leaves the choice to us. He leaves with man the choice of rejecting Jesus Christ or accepting Him. To accept Jesus Christ is to receive right to the tree of life, the city of God, and all the blessings of eternity. To reject Christ is to settle for eternity in the region of the damned. For as surely as there is a heaven, there is a hell. Christ coming back will make that crystal clear. The last dynamic act in history will be the judgment at the great white throne. Only eternity lies beyond that point. Thank God today is still the day of salvation.

12

The New Heavens and the New Earth

The doctrine of last things does not terminate with the great white throne judgment. It stretches across the final convulsions of the present order of things and reaches the shores of eternity. When the first heaven and the first earth have passed away, there must be new heavens and a new earth. The prophetic glimpses of that coming glorious age are few, but they are worthy of the prayerful attention of every child of God. Man's only accurate word about the realities of eternity are to be found in the Scriptures. No other source can speak of eternity with integrity.

In a sphere where things are temporary and constantly changing, where one cycle follows another, it is difficult to think objectively about a state of foreverness. Such a concept is entirely foreign to man's experience here on earth. It is only by divine revelation that the human understanding is opened to things eternal. The apostle Paul, quoting the prophet Isaiah, contrasted the passing wisdom of this age which depends on sight to the wisdom of the God of eternity.

> but just as it is written,
> "Things which eye has not
>   seen and ear has not heard,
> And which have not entered
>   the heart of man,
> All that God has prepared
>   for those who love Him" (1 Cor. 2:9, NASB).

The Holy Spirit, ministering in the church's behalf, draws

aside the veil and offers us those glimpses of eternity necessary to firm our resolve to press toward that city whose builder and maker is God.

The Reality of the New Heavens and New Earth

The new heavens and the new earth will not be an eerie twilight zone, nor some sort of fantasy land. It will be a real place where God dwells with His people. Most believers do not perceive the earth as having any part in eternity. But the Scriptures speak at least five times of a new heavens *and* a new earth.

Paul taught the Ephesians that the earth figures into the purpose of God in Christ.

> *He made known to us the mystery of His will, according to His kind intention which He purposed in Him with a view to an administration suitable to the fulness of the times, that is, the summing up of all things in Christ, things in the heavens and things upon the earth (Eph. 1:9-10, NASB).*

Christ is creator, sustainer, and sovereign of the earth.

> *For by Him all things were created, both in the heavens and on earth, visible and invisible, whether thrones or dominions or rulers or authorities—all things have been created by Him and for Him. And He is before all things and in Him all things hold together (Col. 1:16-17, NASB).*

In these first two passages Paul teaches that the earth has a place in the plan of God. The thrust of redemptive history is toward a new heavens and a new earth where righteousness dwells.

The prophet Isaiah also pictured the new heavens and the new earth, including a new Jerusalem.

> "For behold, I create new heavens and a new
>   earth;
> And the former things shall not be remembered
>   or come to mind.
> But be glad and rejoice forever in what I create;
> For behold, I create Jerusalem for rejoicing,
> And her people for gladness.
> I will also rejoice in Jerusalem,
>   and be glad in My people;
> And there will no longer be heard in her
> The voice of weeping and the sound of crying.
> No longer will there be in it an infant
>   who lives but a few days,
> Or an old man who does not live out his days;
> For the youth will die at the age of
>   one hundred
> And the one who does not reach the age
>   of one hundred
> Shall be thought accursed.
> And they shall build houses and inhabit them;
> They shall also plant vineyards and eat their
>   fruit.
> They shall not build, and another inhabit,
> They shall not plant, and another eat;
> For as the lifetime of a tree, so shall be
>   the days of My people,
> And My chosen ones shall wear out the work of
>   their hands.
> They shall not labor in vain,
> Or bear children for calamity;

For they are the offspring of
  those blessed by the Lord,
And their descendants with them.

It will also come to pass that before they call, I
will answer; and while they are still speaking, I
will hear. The wolf and the lamb shall graze
together and the lion shall eat straw like the ox;
and dust shall be the serpent's food. They shall
do no evil or harm in all My holy mountain," says
the Lord (Isa. 65:17-25, NASB).

The time elements in this passage indicate that Isaiah is
speaking of the millennium, not of the eternal age.
However, Isaiah saw the glad millennial days as a stage in
the prophetic process which ushers in the eternal age. The
millennial reign of Christ is a preview of His eternal reign
in the new heavens and new earth. That which the millennial reign and the eternal reign have in common is the New
Jerusalem, the dwelling place of the saints. Just as the New
Jerusalem will hover over the millennial earth, so it will
hover over the new earth in the age to come.

Isaiah makes a second reference to the new heavens
and the new earth in the closing verses of his prophecy.

"For just as the new heavens
  and the new earth
Which I make will endure before Me,"
  declares the Lord,
"So your offspring and your name will endure.
And it shall be from new moon to new moon
And from sabbath to sabbath,
All mankind will come to bow down before
  Me," says the Lord.
"Then they shall go forth and look

On the corpses of the men
Who have transgressed against Me.
For their worm shall not die,
And their fire shall not be quenched;
And they shall be an abhorrence
   to all mankind" (Isa. 66:22-24, NASB).

The new earth and the new heavens are pictured as existing in eternal blessedness while the wicked endure eternal damnation. Isaiah is saying that the righteous and the damned will have entirely different experiences in eternity. The righteous will live forever in the new order enjoying unbroken and immediate fellowship with God the Father and Jesus Christ the Son and the blessed Holy Spirit. Lost men will endure forever the anguish of hell and the eternal loneliness of separation from God.

Modern evangelicals who are so taken up with the so-called life-related application of Scripture would do well to take a fresh look at these ultimate issues of the gospel. Evangelism ministry, discipleship, and discipline ought always to be considered with eternity in full view.

The fifth passage that pictures the reality of the new heavens and new earth is found in the Book of Revelation. John had the same view of eternity as Isaiah.

And I saw a new heaven and a new earth; for the first heaven and the first earth passed away, and there is no longer any sea. And I saw the holy city, new Jerusalem, coming down out of heaven from God, made ready as a bride adorned for her husband. And I heard a loud voice from the throne saying, "Behold, the tabernacle of God is among men, and He shall dwell among them, and they shall be His people, and God Himself shall be among them, and He shall wipe away every tear from their eyes; and there shall no longer be any death; there shall no longer be any mourning, or crying, or pain; the first things have passed away." And He who sits on the throne said, "Behold, I am making all things new." And He said, "Write, for these words are faithful and true." And He said to me, "It is done. I am the Alpha and the Omega, the beginning and the end. I will give to the one who thirsts from the spring of the water of life without cost. He who overcomes shall inherit these things, and I will be his God and he will be My son. But the cowardly and unbelieving and abominable and murderers and immoral persons and sorcerers and idolators and all liars, their part will be in the lake that burns with fire and brimstone, which is the second death" (Rev. 21:1-8, NASB).

As in Isaiah's vision, the new heavens and earth and the new Jerusalem are pictured first in John's revelation and then the lake of fire, the eternal abode of the ungodly. The biblical doctrine of the restoration of all things contains no hint of universalism. The last biblical pronouncements on eternity declare the reality of both eternal life and eternal damnation.

The Nature of the New Earth

Since the Scriptures, then, tie together the new heavens and the new earth as the dwelling place of God with His people in the eternal age, let us look at the nature of this new earth. First of all, it will be an earth delivered from the curse.

This planet and the material universe that surrounds it were created by God, and His own assessment of that creation was that it was very good. He created the earth with a purpose in view. The achievement of that blessed purpose was interrupted at the fall of man. When God dealt with Adam and Eve He said to them, "Cursed is the ground because of you" (Gen. 3:17, NASB). Deliverance from the curse will be accomplished in the day of the Lord when the new heavens and the new earth come into being. The new order will be a direct result of the triumph of Jesus Christ through His death and resurrection. That great redemptive act broke the curse that tainted the earth because of man's sin.

> For I consider that the sufferings of this present time are not worthy to be compared with the glory that is to be revealed to us. For the anxious longing of the creation waits eagerly for the revealing of the sons of God. For the creation was subjected to futility, not of its own will, but because of Him who subjected it, in hope that the creation itself also will be set free from its slavery to corruption into the freedom of the glory of the children of God. For we know that the whole creation groans and suffers the pains of childbirth together until now. And not only this, but also we ourselves, having the first fruits of the Spirit, even we ourselves groan within ourselves, waiting eagerly for our adoption as sons, the redemption of our body. For in hope we have been saved, but hope that is seen is not hope; for why does one also hope for what he sees? But if we hope for what we do not see, with perseverance we wait eagerly for it (Rom. 8:18-25, NASB).

The groan of creation will be answered by the wonderful

intervention of our returning Lord.

Second, the new earth freed from the curse by Christ will forever be the dwelling place of righteousness. After the final defeat of Satan, God will purge the material universe by fire and bring in the new heavens and the new earth.

> But the day of the Lord will come like a thief, in which the heavens will pass away with a roar and the elements will be destroyed with intense heat, and the earth and its works will be burned up. Since all these things are to be destroyed in this way, what sort of people ought you to be in holy conduct and godliness. Looking for and hastening the coming of the day of God, on account of which the heavens will be destroyed by burning, and the elements will melt with intense heat! But according to His promise we are looking for new heavens and a new earth, in which righteousness dwells (2 Pet. 3:10-13, NASB).

The earth's release from the curse is associated, Paul said in the above passage from Romans, with the glorious release of God's people. The new earth will be all God ever meant the world to be—a place where the presence of God is manifest and righteousness the practice of all its inhabitants.

> And he showed me a river of the water of life, clear as crystal, coming from the throne of God and of the Lamb, in the middle of its street. And on either side of the river was the tree of life, bearing twelve kinds of fruit, yielding its fruit every month; and the leaves of the tree were for

the healing of the nations. And there shall no longer be any curse; and the throne of God and of the Lamb shall be in it, and His bond-servants shall serve Him; and they shall see His face, and His name shall be on their foreheads. And there shall no longer be any night; and they shall not have need of the light of a lamp nor the light of the sun, because the Lord God shall illumine them; and they shall reign forever and ever (Rev. 22:1-5, NASB).

In this passage John addresses the subject of the saints' activity in eternity. There has been a great deal of meaningless sentiment about this aspect of our future, both in the hymns of the church and in preaching. This preview of eternity says nothing of harps, clouds, or angels' robes. God's people are called bond-servants because this name best describes their eternal ministry. The bond-servants of Christ will serve Him forever. Our service now and in the coming kingdom age is only an apprenticeship for service in eternity.

Finally, this new earth is not only delivered from the curse and made the dwelling place of righteousness, it is also brought finally into subjection to its rightful King. In Revelation 22 John picks up again the theme of the kingdom of God. Verse 1 refers to the throne of God and of the Lamb. Verse 5 states that the bond-servants of Christ will reign forever. John's revelation conforms to the vision of the prophets in that it emphasizes the eternal aspect of the kingdom.

The kingdom of Christ extends beyond the thousand-year reign, for the Scriptures speak of it as everlasting. By the same token, the kingdom ministry of redeemed saints will continue beyond the thousand-year reign. The concept of the kingdom must here be related to heaven. Matthew records Jesus' caption for His kingdom as the kingdom of heaven. The millennial manifestation of the kingdom will make real the divine purpose in that the will of God will be done on earth as it is in heaven.

It is in the eternal age that the kingdom will reach its ultimate and everlasting form. The point of triumph described by Paul will be reached.

> Then comes the end, when He delivers up the kingdom to the God and Father, when He has abolished all rule and all authority and power. For He must reign until He has put all His enemies under His feet. The last enemy that will be abolished is death. For He has put all things in subjection under His feet. But when He says, "All things are put in subjection," it is evident that He is excepted who put all things in subjection to Him. And when all things are subjected to Him, then the Son Himself also will be subjected to the One who subjected all things to Him, that God may be all in all (1 Cor. 15:24-28, NASB).

Christ reigns now in the midst of His enemies by governing the hearts of His people. He will reign over the nations of the earth in His millennial kingdom. When the final judgment is over, He will have brought all things under subjection and all His enemies will be under His footstool. Every redemptive preparation will have been completed in anticipation of the dawn of eternity.

The contemplation of eternity is not an easy exercise for mortal man. His whole experience is time-oriented. The realm of eternity lies outside the boundaries of time. The demands of man's natural life and the limitations imposed by its brevity give him little facility for understanding a level of life outside time and nature. Most people never give the subject a serious thought. But to that Spirit-enlightened soul who feeds on the Word of God there comes a yearning for eternity. There comes a decrease in his concern for the needs and the pleasures of this life and an honest reaching out for life in a better world. He comes to associate the full enjoyment of that better land with the coming of Jesus Christ. For when He comes, history as we know it will be terminated and eternity will take its place. The kingdom of God will be on earth as it is in heaven forever and ever.

> O sweet and blessed country, the home of God's elect!
> O sweet and blessed country, that eager hearts expect!
> Jesus, in mercy bring us to that dear land of rest,
> Who art, with God the Father, and Spirit, ever blest.

> They stand, those halls of Zion, all jubilant with song,
> And bright with many an angel, and all the martyr throng.
> There is the throne of David, and there from toil released,
> The shout of them that triumph, the song of them that feast.

> And they who with their leader have conquered in the fight,
> For ever and for ever are clad in robes of white.
> Oh, land that seest no sorrow! oh, state that fear'st no strife!
> Oh, royal land of flowers! oh, realm and home of life!

Jerusalem the glorious, the glory of th' elect,
O dear and future vision that eager hearts expect!
E'en now by faith I see thee, e'en here thy walls
   discern;
To thee my thoughts are kindled, and strive and
   pant and yearn.[1]

---

1. Bernard of Cluny, a twelfth-century Benedictine monk, wrote "The Celestial Country" from which these verses were selected. Parts of this poem sometimes appear in hymnals under the title, "Jerusalem, the Golden." The complete poem can be found in A.W. Tozer's *The Christian's Book of Mystical Verse.* (Harrisburg: Christian Publications, Inc.,) pp. 128-140.

Bibliography

Benson, John L. *The Showdown That Will Rock the World.* Denver: Accent Books, 1977.

Blackstone, William E. *The Millennium.* New York: Revell, 1904.

Boice, James Montgomery. *The Last and Future World.* Grand Rapids: Zondervan, 1974.

Bradbury, John W., ed. *The Sure Word of Prophecy.* New York: Revell, 1943.

Bruce, F. F. *The Time Is Fulfilled.* Grand Rapids: Eerdmans, 1978.

Cumming, John. *The Great Tribulation.* New York: Carleton, 1862.

David, Ira E. *Christ Our Coming King.* Harrisburg, Christian Publications, Inc., 1928.

Feinberg, Charles L. *Millennialism: the Two Major Views.* Chicago: Moody Press, 1980. Revised edition.

_____. ed. *Prophecy and the Seventies.* Chicago: Moody Press, 1971.

Fraser, Alexander. *A Key to the Prophecies of the Old and New Testaments.* Philadelphia: D. Hogan, 1802.

Girdlestone, R. B. *The Grammar of Prophecy.* Grand Rapids: Kregel Publications, 1955.

Gordon, S. D. *Quiet Talks about the Crowned Christ.* New York: Revell, 1914.

Gromacki, Robert Glenn. *Are These the Last Days?* Old Tappan, N. J.: Revell, 1970.

Haldeman, I. M. *The Coming of Christ*. New York: Charles C. Cook, 1906.

Hamilton, Gavin. *Coming Kingdom Glories*. Edinburgh, Scotland: McCall Barber, 1965.

——————.*The Olivet Discourse*. Oak Park: Published by the author, 1960.

—————— . *The Rapture and the Great Tribulation*. New York: Loizeaux Bros., 1957.

Harrison, L. S. *The Remarkable Jew.*, 12th ed. London: Pickering and Inglis.

Inch, Morris A. *Understanding Bible Prophecy*. New York: Harper & Row, 1977.

Koch, Kurt. *Day X*. Grand Rapids: Kregel Publications, 1969.

Ladd, George E. *Jesus and the Kingdom*. Waco: Texas, Word Books Publisher, 1964.

Mackintosh, Charles Henry. *Papers on the Lord's Coming*. Chicago: Moody Press.

MacPherson, Ian. *News of the World to Come*. Sussex, England: Prophetic Witness Publishing House, 1975.

Marsh, F. E. *Why Will Christ Come Back?* Salem: Convention Book Store, (reprint).

Mauro, Philip. *A Kingdom Which Cannot Be Shaken*. Boston: Scripture Truth Depot.

Morgan, G. Campbell. *Behold He Cometh*. New York: Revell, 1912.

Pache, Rene. *The Return of Jesus Christ*. Chicago: Moody Press, 1955.

Payne, J. Barton. *The Imminent Appearing of Christ*. Grand Rapids: Eerdmans, 1962.

Pentecost, J. Dwight. *Things to Come*. Findley, Ohio: Durham, 1958.

Pettingill, William. *Israel—Jehovah's Covenant People*. Wilmington: Just A Word.

Pink, Arthur W. *The Millennium*. Swengel, Pa.: Bible Truth Depot.

_____ . *The Redeemer's Return*. Swengel, Pa.: Bible Truth Depot, 1918.

Second Coming of Christ, The. A compilation. Chicago: The Bible Institute Colportage Association, 1896.

Silver, Jesse Forrest. *The Lord's Return*. 7th ed. New York: Revell, 1914.

Simpson, A. B. *The Gospel of the Kingdom*. New York: Christian Alliance Publishing Co., 1890.

_____ . *The Coming One*. New York: Christian Alliance Publishing Co., 1912.

_____ . *Back to Patmos*. New York: Christian Alliance Publishing Co., 1914.

Schlink, Basilea. *For Jerusalem's Sake I Will Not Rest*. London: England, Evangelical Sisterhood, 1971.

Smith, Wilbur M. *Egypt in Biblical Prophecy*. Boston: W. A. Wilde, 1957.

_____ . *Israeli-Arab Conflict and the Bible*. Glendale: Regal, 1967.

_____ . *This Atomic Age and the Word of God*. Boston: W. A. Wilde, 1948.

Stevens, W. C. *Revelation, the Crown Jewel of Prophecy*, vol. 2. Harrisburg, Pennsylvania: Christian Publications, Inc. Reprint of 1928 edition.

Telfer, John. *The Coming Kingdom of God*. London: Marshall Brothers.

Walvoord, John F. *Armegeddon, Oil and the Middle East Crisis*. Grand Rapids: Zondervan, 1974.

_____ . *The Millennial Kingdom*. Grand Rapids: Zondervan, 1980.

West, Nathanael. *The Thousand Years in Both Testaments*. Fincastle, Virginia: Scripture Book. Reprint of 1889 edition.

White, John Wesley. *Re-entry*. Grand Rapids: Zondervan, 1970.

Scripture Index

General Index